How to KEEP a Woman Happy

A Collage of Stories About the Women

Who Had Their Way with Me

by Bret A McClanahan

DORRANCE
PUBLISHING CO
EST. 1920
PITTSBURGH, PENNSYLVANIA 15238

Dorrance Publishing Co
585 Alpha Drive
Pittsburgh, PA 15238
Visit our website at dorrancebookstore.com

ISBN: 978-1-6461-0522-9
eISBN: 978-1-6461-0658-5

Dedicated to Minami…
YSC! And YOU "Still" know why…and YOU always will.

ASTUTE, AS-TUTE, adjective
"Having or showing an ability to accurately assess situations or people and turn this to one's advantage." — Google

"Why should the Kardashians have all the fun? We should all strive to live like Kourtney and her sisters." — Bret A McClanahan

After President Obama said on TV that little American girls should not watch the Kardashians because they are not real...

Chapter One
Bail Her Out

It was summer in Albuquerque and the sky was so blue it was as if we lived above the world. I was driving east and had just crossed the Rio Grande over the Montano Bridge when I caught the red light on Fourth Street. It has been so many years now I do not recall where I was driving...perhaps New Mexico Plaster and Supply, since they were just a few blocks south on Fourth and it was my job to represent a company that manufactured stucco.

When my cell phone rang, and I did not see the ever-popular 505 New Mexico area code, I was compelled to answer. The phone was primarily for business use anyway, and it was provided by my corporate office, and they paid the bill each month anyway.

"Hello! This is Bret. How can we help you?" I answered super excited and enthusiastic like an AM radio personality. People often comment on my telephone demeanor.

A hysterical young woman crying and talking a mile a minute was on the line. "Oh Bret...I am so glad that it's *you*...You do not know me... I am Patty, Rachel's friend, and there was a fight. She was arrested. She is in jail, and her only call was to me, and I missed the call and she left a voicemail with your number and said *you* would know what to do!"

I remained calm, cool, and collected like George Clooney in his movies.

"In Dallas?" I asked.

"Yes!" replied Patty, still crying and hysterical. "Rachel was arrested for fighting at around 2:00 A.M."

YSC! You're So Cool...

As the light changed to green and I proceeded east on Montano, I said to Patty, "Okay, relax. I was a bar and restaurant manager way back in the twentieth century, and I have bailed out oodles of people. We can get through this but, Patty..."

"Yes," Patty said, now a bit calmer and only sobbing and not crying.

"Stay calm and cool with me all right?" I was speaking softly, almost in a whisper.

"Okay," Patty answered. "It's just that I missed her call, and she is my best friend and I want to get her out of jail."

"I understand, Patty," I continued. "Are you on a lunch break? Dallas is an hour ahead of Albuquerque."

"Yes," answered Patty, now very reserved and understanding that I would assist her to bail out Rachel from jail in Dallas.

"Fine," I responded. "This will take a few hours—not like in the movies. Call your boss...*You* will need the rest of the day off."

"Oh *no!*" Patty began crying in hysterics, again falling to pieces. "I can't do this..."

I remained calm and cool, but stern. "Patty, Patty...breath. *We* are going to bail out Rachel. This just takes time. Let me drive to my corporate office only a few blocks away and get in contact with a Dallas bail bond place."

"Okay," Patty said, sobbing again and a bit more in control.

I verified her number on my caller ID and instructed Patty to call her boss and say she was sick. "Do *not* tell the truth that you have enlisted the help of a man you never met in Albuquerque to bail out your best friend Rachel from a Dallas jail for fighting at 2:00 A.M. My mind was racing as I drove to my corporate office. I knew my boss Richard was out of town in Colorado and our CFO was also out of the office. Lola the office manager would not pay attention to what I was doing, and I could sneak into the private conference room and use that phone if needed. I was driving a sweet '95 Tahoe at the time with American racing rims and a cool black leather bra bug deflector on the hood. The vehicle was a sort of champagne color (GM Autumn Wood) and had a mean sounding engine. As I raced into the parking lot, it appeared that a number of people from my corporate office were already at lunch. So, cool...I would have some privacy. Via the magic of the internet, I found a reasonable bail bonds location in Dallas. When I called them, they told me the bail was set for Rachel at five hundred dollars cash, and since the number was so low, they advised I wire the money using Western Union to a friend in Dallas. The bail man was super cool and confirmed where Rachel was held...some yadda yadda municipal jail in Dallas. I thanked him for the information and called Patty.

"Okay, so here is the deal, "I started to explain to Patty. "I am going to wire *you* five hundred bucks through Western Union, and *you* take the cash and bail out Rachel."

Patty fell apart again, crying and losing control. "Oh my God... I can't do this!"

I jumped in, George Clooney calm, cool and stern. "Patty...*We* can do this. I possess a BA in Fine Arts from The Colorado College in Colorado Springs. This is *no* big deal."

"Okay," Patty said, calmed down yet again. "What do I need to do?"

I instructed Patty, "I will wire five hundred dollars cash with Western Union and you go to a Kmart or Albertson's Super Market customer service desk. The password will be "Rachel," and you will need to show your ID. Ask for large bills, like fifties or hundreds. Stick it in your pocket right away and then drive directly to the jail and let them know *you* are there with *cash* to bail out Rachel."

About thirty minutes later, Patty called excited and told me she had the money and was on her way to bail out Rachel from jail.

"I know, Patty," I said, nice and calm. "Western Union sent a text confirmation that Patty has the five hundred bucks. Go get your best friend Rachel out of jail and call me later. Know and understand, this will take a long time."

Several hours passed, and I had a productive day representing the stucco company where I was employed. Later that evening, while relaxing on my green L-shaped sofa sectional in my mid-century modern living room with dry-stack-ledge stone wall all the way to the top of the vaulted ceiling, my phone rang, and the caller ID displayed that it was Rachel. I did not answer and let it go to voicemail.

It was Rachel on the voicemail, and she was crying. "I knew you could help, me Bret, and that is why I told Patty to call. I will pay back every bit of the five hundred bucks as soon as I can, and *you* know that I am good for it."

The next day, I told Lola, our office manager, what had transpired the day before.

"You are crazy and *you* will never see a dime of the five hundred dollars you sent to bail her out," Lola scolded me.

Over the course of the next few weeks, about three different times I got a bubble-wrap envelope with cash from Rachel, a Hallmark card, and a CD with music from Xtina Aguilera or Fergie. I dumped out the contents on Lola's desk each time I received the parcel from Rachel.

"Get that glitter stripper money off my desk, Bret!" Lola would yell. "It's filthy."

Remind me later to tell how I met Rachel in Albuquerque before she moved to Dallas.

Chapter Two
Rescue Her (with the Spare Key FOB)

My favorite little Asian (as she described herself) Minami had lived with me for nearly a year. It was February, and she had almost completed her three BA degrees from the University of New Mexico in Entrepreneurship, Business, and Finance. Minami wanted to be a patent lawyer, and she boasted constantly. "Well Bret, *you* are stuck with me for at least three more years while I attend UNM Law School." Minami was also finished with the bulking portion of her fitness competition training and was now starting the cutting.

"Hey Bret," Minami would always say with her perpetual smile. "Would you like to see the posing I am required to do for the fitness competition in June?"

"Only if you wear a bikini or *the* actual bikini for the competition itself," I would reply, calm and cool.

I had purchased a bad-ass Range Rover the year before on my lunch hour in what the salesman said was the fastest sale he ever had accomplished. The black Range Rover Sport looked like the one driven by Kendall Jenner, and after I had put on some Yokohama tires, custom black rims from California, and dark tinted windows, it was no wonder that Minami made the beast her own. I had placed Minami on my car insurance to cover her on the Range Rover Sport HSE, the big nasty yellow H2 Hummer, as well as the all-black Chevy Tahoe with old-school chrome rims. To complete the Range Rover, I had a "New Mexico: Chile Capital of the World" license plate with AS-TUTE stamped. Vanity plates in New Mexico are not too expensive, and the state only issues a single plate for the rear of the vehicle.

Minami was freaking cool and sort of validation for my alpha-male status. She still worked a couple nights per week at Twin Peaks, and we had a super blast living together. She spent a huge amount of time with her face in a book, on her Apple laptop computer, or at the gym in preparation for her fitness competition. She and I ate super healthy, making baked sweet potato slices with Himalayan pink salt, cinnamon, and paprika as I had seen on a YouTube video covering the diet of Ariana Grande. As an Instagram model with well over twenty-one thousand followers, Minami had all sorts of sponsors sending FedEx packages to the house with gym clothes and such. She even had a food sponsor, vitamin supplement sponsor, teeth-whitening sponsor…Ugh, I could go on. I spent a fortune on cool Nike stuff and yet had no reason since she had so much clothes.

We watched a lot of the TV show *Shark Tank* on MSNBC when there were marathon days, as well as *Keeping Up with the Kardashians* on E! Minami just concentrated on her studies and gym workouts in November and December, and I probably had the most memorable Christmas season ever with her. We watched the movie *Crazy Rich Asians* on Xfinity on Demand and laughed our asses off.

Minami followed Buff Bunny Heidi Sommers on Instagram, and I watched a lot of the Buff Bunny videos on YouTube. Heidi Sommers drove a bad-ass Mercedes Benz all-black G-Wagon, and I kept teasing Minami that I wanted to replace the Range Rover Sport with a White G-Wagon. I even sent her via text message G-Wagons in the Scottsdale area that could easily ship to Albuquerque.

At the last minute I had to travel for an all-day trip to Carlsbad and look at some cracks in stucco since our technical representative flaked at the last minute. Minami had mentioned that she planned to stay home all day and study, with the exception of a couple hours in the gym during the morning. Since it was the day before Valentine's Day, I had made special arrangements with People's Flowers in Albuquerque to deliver a big-ass arrangement of white roses to Minami and another separate arrangement of red roses. I lied to Minami and explained that I was expecting a FedEx package that required a signature and that she would need to be home for me. Everything worked out so well

YSC! You're So Cool.

During the long-ass drive back home to Albuquerque, Minami sent me a text with a picture of her People's Flowers, which confirmed the delivery to my house. I explained that I had another surprise and that I was rushing to get home.

Minami accused me of traveling to Scottsdale for a G-Wagon purchase and not for Carlsbad to look at stucco cracks for work. Minami was hired to be in a T-Pain music video, which was scheduled to shoot in the wee hours of that night/early morning in Santa Fe at Meow Wolf. When I arrived home, Minami was in her tiny gym shorts and a T shirt, bare footed, and at the conference table I use for a dining room table with her Apple laptop computer.

"I am so glad that *you* are still here," I said. "What time do you need to be in Santa Fe?"

Minami replied with a twinkle in her eye and that same ever-present smile. "Not sure if I want to do this. They will film the video all night. I want to get a hotel room but don't want to stay alone in Santa Fe."

7

"I would be happy to tag along if You want, and get a hotel room, or drive you back to Albuquerque in the morning," I told Minami, and then I added, "You may want to get ready if you are going…It takes at least an hour to drive from here to Santa Fe."

"I know," said Minami again with a happy smile and positive mood.

"Throw on some flip flops and come outside to the driveway," I said laughing. "I have your Valentine's present."

"Shut up!" Minami exclaimed as she put flip flops for her bare feet. "Did you drive to Scottsdale and get a G-Wagon?"

I made Minami cover her eyes as we navigated through the garage past the big nasty yellow H2 Hummer and "her" Range Rover.

"Okay," I said. "Open your eyes."

Minami laughed at the tiny white die-cast model replica white Mercedes Benz G-Wagon with shiny red bow in the driveway. She ran over and picked up the toy, laughing. One can purchase anything on Amazon, even a tiny replica Mercedes Benz G-Wagon. She would then shower, put on her makeup, get dressed, and drive to Santa Fe at 10:30 P.M.

I told her, "You are so spoiled, and I hope they still allow you to be in the video, going so late. It will be near midnight when you arrive in Santa Fe."

Minami just snickered and gave me a sexy look.

I have always had the ability to wake super stupid early each morning just before 5:00 A.M. I set my alarm but usually wake before the clock tells me to get my ass out of bed. Minami was impressed with my abilities, and she had been working on getting up when I did or at least when I departed from the house at 6:30 A.M. to start my day representing the stucco company where I am employed.

Valentine's was no exception. Just before 6:00 A.M. after I had performed duties on my computer, checking sales numbers, and logging calls on our CRM, I noticed a text message from Minami.

"The Range Rover Key FOB is dead."

I called Minami right away. "No big deal. I can bring you the spare. Just give me about an hour."

Her voice was very sweet and calm, just like the introverted, Instagram model, half-Japanese half-Italian, Twin Peaks studious, UNM pre-law student she was. "I knew I could count on you Bret. See you in an hour."

In the all-black Chevy Tahoe with cool shiny, old-school, chrome rims, I rapidly drove up Interstate-25 to Santa Fe. I thought about how super cool the Range Rover dealer in Albuquerque was the previous August when I had purchased a spare key FOB and had them program the device. They had big fat comfy leather chairs and dry-stack ledge stone in a mid-century modern motif. A sexy young woman in business attire pointed out coffee and snacks. Sure was glad I decided to be proactive and get the very expensive spare key FOB for "her" Range Rover with "New Mexico: Chile Capital of the World" plates with ASTUTE stamped on them.

As the sun was beginning to rise over the Sandia Mountains, I came back to reality and stopped thinking about how cool the Range Rover dealer is in Albuquerque and how near the Range Rover dealer is in Santa Fe. Oh man, reality was really setting in at about that moment...As I exited Interstate-25 onto Cerrillos Road in Santa Fe, my first thought was...*Oh fawk!* Certainly the Range Rover dealer tested the key FOB after it was programmed..." My mind was racing, as I knew I was ten minutes away from rescuing Minami in Santa Fe at the T-Pain music video shoot at Meow Wolf. This damn key FOB better work.

As I rambled into the parking lot at Meow Wolf, there were the ever-present electrical cords and trailers and such associated with a video shoot. The Range Rover, "her" Range Rover, was parked all alone, sad and cold. There was a white minivan of sorts, parked near.

No sign of Minami, and it was cold outside…Hey, it was February 14 and the crack of dawn.

I parked next to "her" Range Rover and immediately used the key FOB to unlock the doors. *Voilà!* The lights came on. Yes!

Minami had been waiting in the white minivan with the producer and staff. She got out, approached me, gave me a big super-squeeze hug and a sincere kiss on my jaw standing on her tiptoes, since I am a giant next to her. She pressed against me so tight, like a James Bond villain. "Did you have a good time?" I asked. "What was the *best* part about shooting a T-Pain music video?"

"Oh my God, yes," Minami said with a twinkle in her eye and big movie-star smile. "Everything happens for a reason, Bret. Just like the law of attraction. Being stranded here gave me quality time to potentially get cast in more music videos. I visited with the producer and director…provided my Instagram."

"You're so cool Minami!" I exclaimed. "Hand over the dead key FOB, and I can get the battery replaced today. Drive safe getting home, and I will see *you* later tonight."

I had provided Minami with my Wells Fargo Platinum card the previous summer when she turned twenty-one so she could get breast augmentation surgery with the instructions to not go over ten grand. The Range Rover Sport, new boobs, and just having a blast living with Bret in his cool mid-century modern homemade Minami a very happy woman, and she reminded me of that fact often. She would bring fried chicken strips tossed in spicy Thai sauce from Twin Peaks often and put it in my giant double-door stainless-steel monster fridge with a note on small yellow paper: "YSC! You're So Cool! YFA" YFA means your favorite Asian. I was Minami's hero, and bringing her the spare key FOB for "her" Range Rover at the crack of dawn in Santa Fe at the T-Pain music video shoot was just another chapter in the long line of Minami stories.

About a month later I was relaxing on the green L-shaped sofa sectional in my mid-century, modern living room with dry-stacked-ledge stone all the way up the wall to the vaulted ceiling, watching music videos on BET Jams. Bang! There it was. The T-Pain music video shot at Meow Wolf in Santa Fe with Minami.

I sat up, excited. "Hey Minami, get out here...*You* are on TV... It's the T-Pain video."

She was in the spare bedroom used as an office working on a class project.

"Yeah okay," she said, calm and humble. "Can you take a picture with your smart phone?"

To this day I cannot even tell you if Minami has watched that T-Pain video...even on YouTube.

That is what I love about Minami...she is always so matter-of-fact, calm, and humble living like one of those Kardashian sisters... even driving a cool Range Rover Sport just like a Kardashian sister.

Why should only the Kardashians have so much fun? If the Kardashians are doing it...it must be fun!

We should all strive to live a life just like Kourtney and her sisters.

I must admit, I look forward being "stuck" with Minami for at least three more years while she attends UNM Law School.

Chapter Three
Wash Her Range Rover

I had actually met Minami while she was working a shift at Twin Peaks in Albuquerque on the Saturday after Valentine's a year before her T-Pain music video shoot. We hit it off. She started driving the Range Rover Sport I had purchased. She was my house sitter while I had a business meeting in Dallas, and she subsequently moved all of her stuff into my home and became my house guest, whereupon we had numerous adventures.

Several years before I met Minami, however, I met a woman named Rose at the Hooters location on San Mateo in Albuquerque, and she too had a sweet black Range Rover Sport. I had a cool friend named Felicia who helped serve beer at our hospitality tent each summer for the Home Builders Association of Central New Mexico Golf Benefit. That big stucco company where I represent…Yeah…a major sponsor for that golf benefit every year. Roxy also came a couple non-consecutive years to serve beer with Felicia. Felicia worked at Hooters, and she was a University of New Mexico Student. I think her major was communications, and that is why she knew American Sign Language. Anyway…I used to do laundry on Saturday mornings, and Felicia would either call or text and let me know that if I got her a Kiva Juice and I got Roxy a Chi Tea from Starbucks, those women would purchase my lunch at Hooters. Felicia and Roxy always worked the patio area.

After picking up their beverages from Kiva Juice and Starbucks, I would then text Felicia my order…chicken quesadillas and a side of guacamole. Bang! Everything was ready upon my arrival, and I would hang on the patio at Hooters on San Mateo in Albuquerque on Saturday with Felicia and Roxy. Often, I would bring a Victoria's Secret catalog and all the Hooters women would visit my table to look and dream about purchases. There was an issue of *Playboy* magazine with an interview with Bill Richardson, governor of New Mexico and a convenient pictorial of a nude Kim Kardashian. Roxy resembled Kim, but not as voluptuous. Yeah, that was a very memorable day when I had that issue of *Playboy* at my table. Never one to bring a wing man, I rather chose a Victoria's Secret catalog, an issue of Playboy, or some other periodical that would draw attention from the Hooters servers.

Felicia drove a cool, new Mustang panty dropper, and Roxy drove a pearl-white Caddy Escalade. For those of you who do not know, some women who work at places like Hooters or Twin Peaks are smart, and they make a butt load of money. Always parked beside Roxy's Escalade was a sleek, black Range Rover Sport with New York plates. Felicia and Roxy explained to me that the Range Rover was driven by Rose, an exotic young Puerto Rican woman with caramel skin, jet-black hair in a near Afro, and green eyes…I swear she had green eyes. Why would I make that up?

I had recently purchased my big, nasty yellow H2 Hummer in July because I loved the hit TV show *Entourage* on HBO, and I had to drive a Hummer just like those guys on the show. I remember Roxy and Felicia going outside to take a look at my beast. Felicia was at the front passenger door and Roxy at the rear door, both standing on their tiptoes so they could get a good peek inside. Their tight little butts looked so nice in their orange HOOTER uniform shorts. *That* is certainly a picture I wish I had taken…but my memory will need to do and *you* must take my word for it. Oh yeah, it was an amazing sight.

YSC ! You're So Cool.

Anyway…I kind of need to get back on track. Rose was a friend of Roxy's, and it was explained to me that her boyfriend was a stockbroker or lawyer. Hell, I cannot recall since it has been so many years. Apparently, this boyfriend provided the Range Rover for Rose and that is why there were New York plates. I had a super crush on Rose from the start…tiny petite, caramel skin, jet-black hair in a near Afro, great movie star smile, and oh yes…green eyes…Why would I make that up?

I even took Janet from accounts receivable from the big stucco company corporate office to lunch at Hooters one day to verify how pretty Rose appeared. Janet gave me proper validation about Rose when she said, "Wow…You have the most pretty green eyes." Rose smiled and gave me a sexy look.

On one particular Saturday, Hooters on San Mateo was extra busy and crowded , leaving no open tables in the patio area. Rose was working the bar and all alone. I sat at the bar, and she flirted and teased me about how ugly she felt my big nasty yellow H2 Hummer looked.

I had brought a standard juice from Kiva for Felicia and a chi tea for Roxy. I had mentioned to Felicia, "Damn, that Roxy has movie star teeth…so white, straight, and amazing."

"Oh yeah, "Felicia agreed. "Roxy drinks everything with a straw and brushes her teeth like four times per day. I am going to *tell* Roxy what *you* have said about her 'movie star' teeth! That will make her day, since most guys only notice her big fake boobs."

"Roxy has fake boobs?" I started to laugh uncontrollably. "Wow…Here I am with a BA in Fine Arts from The Colorado College and even with her tight white Hooters uniform tank, I never noticed her boobs."

Felicia laughed and punched me hard in the shoulder. "Yeah, right…Whatever Bret."

Yes, as I may have mentioned before, Roxy resembled Kim Kardashian but more athletic and not quite as plump. I would say she looked more like Nichol Scherzinger from The Pussycat Dolls.

"Don't Cha Wish Yer Girlfriend Was HOT Like Me?"

Roxy came up to me sitting at the bar area and gave me one of those half hug deals, placing her head on my shoulder, and with her deep brown eyes, looked directly at me and whispered, "That was so nice of you to notice my smile."

This action caught the attention of Rose who, working the bar, walked down to where I was seated.

"Ugh!" Rose gagged. "How can You drive that ugly yellow truck?"

I had brought a Victoria's Secret catalog that day, and Rose and I were glancing through looking at women in underwear in between her pouring beers behind the bar for the other women servers on the patio and dining area. Rose had mentioned she wanted to study fine arts.

"I have a BA in fine arts!" I yelled, surprised. "Did Felicia or Roxy tell you?"

We were having such a good time visiting and getting to know each other better. Rose knew a lot about the Victoria's Secret models depicted on the pages of the catalog. "Oh yeah, she is so and so, and she dates the guy who plays for yadda yadda NBA team. He gave her a forty-five-thousand-dollar ring and a Rolex."

Then suddenly I sprang into action with a unique opportunity. I noticed a young woman in the Victoria's Secret catalog who closely resembled Rose. "Who is this model?"

"Hm…" Rose replied. "I don't think she is anyone famous…yet."
Rose got a few drink order tickets in and had to once again pour beers
for the other women servers at Hooters on San Mateo in Albuquerque
on that particular busy Saturday.

"I thought this woman in the catalog was *you*, Rose," I said, ex-
tremely serious and calm like George Clooney acts in his movies.

Rose rolled her eyes and walked away for a minute, "Yeah, I am a
Victoria's Secret model and I still work a shift at Hooters on Saturday."

"I have a sweet idea Rose," I continued without skipping a beat.
"You should give me the keys to that Range Rover."

"What the hell? Why would you need the keys to the Range
Rover?" asked Rose, laughing.

"To top off the tank with gas and run it through the car wash for
you," I answered. "Now hurry up and get me those keys before I
change my mind."

Rose departed the bar area and was gone for a few minutes. All
I could think was, "Stupid pick-up line…You blew it…She will not
return."

Around the corner and back behind the bar, Rose approached me
with a giant jumble of keys and some sort of fuzzy key ring deal that
looked like a Tribble from the original Captain Kirk and Mr. Spock
1960s-era *Star Trek* TV series. I think it was purple, if memory serves.

"Don't go very far, Bret." Rose said as she handed me the glob of
keys and the Tribble Star Trek thing, "And don't be gone too long."

"Are you working a double shift?" I asked, surprised now that I
had the Range Rover keys and at a loss for words.

"Yes," Rose answered. "but so what? Don't go very far and don't
be gone too long."

Pardon my French, but I was so fawking excited. I ran out to the
patio and told Roxy and Felicia that Rose had given me her Range
Rover keys and that I was off to wash her machine.

"What?" Felicia exclaimed confused. "Why do you want to wash her Range Rover?"

Once inside the Range Rover, I could not determine where the ignition was located. Ah ha! In the center console next to the gear shift. The inside of the Range Rover was immaculate and smelled like the perfume of a beautiful woman. I drove slowly and cautiously up San Mateo to Academy where there was a Phillips 66 gas station complete with a car wash right across from Trombino's Italian. Rose had more than half a tank of fuel, so I did not spend much topping off her tank, and then went through the Ultimate Automatic car wash. Oh and yeah…it took me a few minutes to figure out where the gas nozzle was located and then how to open it on the Range Rover. Never told anyone that detail before because I was such an alpha male that day. Now the world knows that I took Rose's Range Rover to Phillips 66 and almost could not figure out how to pump gas. On the drive back, I stopped at Pep Boys on San Mateo to get a spray can of that stuff that makes the tires shine like a dealer showroom. I started to think. *Someone said her real name is Ingrid but she goes by Rose. She is Puerto Rican from New York, and her last name starts with Z? Yeah, Okay…this may get screwy if I get stopped by the police.* I suddenly thought about those real life shows on TV like *Cops* or *Real Stories of The Highway Patrol.*

"Serious, Officer, she is tending bar right now just down the street at Hooters. She goes by Rose, and I have no idea why this Range Rover has New York plates or who owns the vehicle. I left my Hummer at Hooters. I just wanted to top off her gas tank and wash it for her."

Using my powers from the Law of Attraction, I was able to park right smack in the front of Hooters by the door, which was very unusual since the joint was so stupid crazy busy that particular Saturday.

I went in through the patio and again took ten tons of shit from Felicia and Roxy. "What the hell did you just do? You washed that Range Rover for Rose…*and* you put gas in it.?"

Rose and I became pretty good friends after I washed her Range Rover. We met for lunch at Azuma for Sushi, and when she left Hooters to be a server at Nob Hill Bar and Grill, she would Text me when she was working so I could come in and sit in her section. I made my associate Evan meet me at Nob Hill Bar and Grill once for happy hour so he could meet Rose, the former Hooters server presently driving a Range Rover. I had known Evan since I first moved to Albuquerque as a Bennigan's manager when Evan was a bartender. Evan became a real estate agent and sold me a home that became my mid-century modern cool pad with Zen garden and Koi pond in the back and dry-stack-ledge-stone on the wall all the way up the vaulted ceiling in the living room.

"Why are we here?" Evan asked. "Who is this Rose? You washed her Range Rover and put gas in it?"

"Evan," I continued. "Hot women also have hot friends, and they all talk. Should anything develop with Rose and her Range Rover… great! If not, I know she will always have nice things to say about Bret."

Chapter Four
The Importance of Business Cards

I was having lunch one day at Hooters with an associate named Marcos from the same company. He represented tile grout and setting material while I represented stucco. Our job was kind of like the Tom Cruise movie *Jerry Maguire* where Tom is a pro sports agent. I represented a corporation that manufactured stucco, and it was my task to bring the distributors of our stucco together with applicators and seal big deals. I was responsible for a few million dollars in sales per year. We had a super team at that office, and those are some of the best years of my life. We wore nice business attire...slacks and dress shirts. I liked to wear nice polished cowboy boots, black slacks in the winter, khaki slacks in the summer, with Ralph Lauren Oxford dress shirts either from the Ralph Lauren Outlets in Santa Fe or Macy's online during after-Christmas or Father's Day Sales. (Secret: Most of my black dress slacks are actually Dickies work pants. Using an X-acto knife, I carefully cut off the Dickies tag and have them pressed at the dry cleaner. Sweet pants.)

We often entertained applicators and distributors to big power lunches, and we participated in all sorts of golf benefits and other events. I served on numerous boards of directors, such as the Santa

Fe Area Home Builders, The Home Builders Association of Central New Mexico, Women's Housing Coalition, Remodeler's Council, Green Build New Mexico, Albuquerque Mayor's Green Task Force, and my favorite…the New Mexico Bio Park, where I served a cool six-year term meeting at the Rio Grande Zoo in Albuquerque.

We had an expense account for travel and entertainment…

Anyway, back to lunch with Marcos at Hooters on San Mateo in Albuquerque. I had noticed a new girl across the dining area who resembled Lisa Bonet, who played Denise on *The Cosby Show* way back in the twentieth century. This woman even sort of had an afro hairstyle. I asked our server to bring the new girl to our table, and I read "Phoenix" that was printed across her white tank Hooters uniform.

"Yes, I just moved here from Phoenix, where I was working at Hooters and dropped out of ASU," she told me, making eye contact with a big movie-star smile. "My name is Rachel." (*See*, I told you I would explain how I met Rachel before she moved from Albuquerque to Dallas and I assisted her best friend Patty to bail her out of jail.)

"Very cool to meet you, Rachel," I said as confidently as I could. "My name is Bret, and if you need anyone to show you around Albuquerque, I am your man."

"Well, thanks, but I have a boyfriend," Rachel answered.

As Rachel walked away looking back at me, our server said, laughing, "She does *not* have a boyfriend."

About a week later, Marcos and I again met at Hooters on San Mateo, but this time for happy hour after work. Our corporate office was nearby, and I wanted to see this Rachel woman again. Home run! Just as is the case with the Law of Attraction, Rachel was indeed our server. We were drinking pitchers of Bud Light and eating buffalo shrimp. While Marcos excused himself to go to the parking lot to take a phone call away from the bar noise of Hooters, I got up the nerve to talk to Rachel.

"Why did you ask to see my ID when I ordered the beer?" I asked.

"We are required to see everyone's ID" Rachel answered.

"I am that dork who asked to show you around Albuquerque last week," I said back to her.

Rachel answered with, "You don't look like a dork to me." She then went to tend another one of the tables in her section.

When she returned, Rachel asked, "Where is your friend? Is he coming back? I cannot leave a pitcher of beer on the table if you are alone."

"He is just outside on the phone," I answered. "Forget about my friend...Do you still have that boyfriend?"

"Yes I do, "Rachel told me. "I live with him." And again she went to tend another table in her section.

Marcos returned and said he would need to leave to pick up someone from the airport. He tossed me some cash to pay his share, and off he went. Rachel returned and offered another pitcher of Bud Light. I said yes, and she returned with a fresh cold, foamy golden pitcher.

"Let me give you my business card." I handed my card to Rachel. "Put that on your refrigerator at home, and if that boyfriend gets jealous and buys you flowers...he is a keeper. If he doesn't do anything, *you* need to call me and I will meet *you* for lunch."

Rachel silently placed the card in her money pouch and looked me in the eye as she smiled and nodded her head in the international "yes" up-and-down motion. I started to feel tipsy from all the beer and called Lola, our office manager, to see if she could give me a ride home. It was a couple hours since work for the day had ended, and I knew Lola was already home. She agreed to swing by Hooters and get me but stated that it would be at least another hour. As I waited for Lola, the big African, shaved-head Hooters manager kept coming to my table and rapping his hand asking, "Hey chief...you okay? Shall we call safe ride services or a cab for you?"

Rachel told me not to worry, that she was off by 9:00 P.M., and she would drive me home. WTF...serious...A Hooters server is going to drive me home after over-serving me? Really, is this happening? In a panic I sent Lola a text. "Are YOU on your WAY?"

When Lola arrived, there were about six Hooters servers at my table, and they had all autographed a Hooters T shirt. They all split and ran when Lola arrived, and the sight of their tight little butts in those tiny orange uniform Hooters shorts was a memorable sight. I had recently ended a fling with Rajah, a very attractive African American woman, and I think I was rushing things with the Lisa Bonet look-a-like Rachel at Hooters. Remind me to tell you about Rajah later.

It was over a full week later when Dave, Mark, Marcos, and I were standing in our corporate office parking lot at the big stucco company trying to figure out what to do about lunch when my cell phone rang. "Good Morning, this is Bret. How can we help you?" Yes, once again all excited and enthusiastic like an AM radio personality.

In her soft sexy, confident voice she whispered, "Hello Bret, this is Rachel. They had enough girls to work today, and I was cut (from the schedule), and I was wondering if you would like to meet me for crab legs?"

Whoa, is this shit really happening?

"Of course Rachel!" I responded. "I would love to join you for lunch."

She informed me that she was at home and wanted to freshen up and suggested that we just meet back at Hooters in about thirty minutes. Marcos and the guys would *not* come with me. "You are on your own dude," Marcos said as he, Dave, and Mark went to Billy's Longbar or some other place for lunch.

As I sat on the hardwood stool at Hooters Rachel entered the bar in tiny booty shorts and a tight blue tank with her fuzzy afro pouring out from under a travel cap. She looked like a woman in a movie, big

smile and all. She was direct with eye contact. We ordered crab legs…
a big ridiculous pile of crab legs.

"You know that boyfriend I live with?" Rachel asked, starting to
build a rapport.

"Yes," I answered with a squeaky voice, as if I had just begun pu-
berty…damn hot butter from the crab legs.

"Well," Rachel started as she wiggled and placed her hands on
the stool between her legs. "I don't really have a boyfriend."

The testosterone shot through my body like a bolt of lightning
and now I too needed to adjust my seat on the hard wood stool at
Hooters. I sat up straight. "Really…no boyfriend?"

"No boyfriend." Rachel said, abrupt and to the point in an official tone.

"That is good to know," I said. "I guess you did not need to place
my business card on your refrigerator, but I am glad you used the card
to secure my number and call me."

Rachel looked me directly in the eye and ran her tongue across
her plump lips, shiny with gloss. "There is *no* boyfriend…but I have
a girlfriend, and I live with her."

"Wow…okay. I see." The wind was out of my sails at this point.
I did manage to smile and keep eye contact, as this was getting in-
teresting.

"I do go out with guys sometimes, and I hope you don't see anything wrong with all of this." Rachel smiled back at me.

"No not at all." I replied. "Will we need to be discrete and keep
this all from your girlfriend?"

"Yes," Rachel answered. "*We* will need to keep this secret. One
more thing. I dropped out of ASU in Phoenix."

"I remember that. You told me already." I said.

"Well, I did not just transfer to Albuquerque with Hooters." Rachel began. "I also dance at TD's Gentlemen's Club and sometimes
at Knockouts. Since Hooters did not need me today, I was thinking

of picking up a shift at Knockouts this afternoon, and *you* could be my customer, Bret, in the VIP lounge."

"Your customer? Naw, I have a lot of work today," I said.

"Aw Bret, come on. It will be so much fun. We can get drunk. I will dance all day for *you* in our private area, except once an hour when I need to dance on stage. Please Bret, it will be so much fun." Rachel was speaking softly in a whisper and still making eye contact with me.

"Since I have a BA in Fine Arts, I have college credit for looking at nude women." I smarted off, "And I only make schoolteacher wages, so I don't have *that* kind of money to spend." I tried my best not to laugh.

"What a drag. Bret, we will have so much fun, and I bet you make a lot of money."

I did *not* go watch her dance that day. I did, however, ask if she could serve beer at the golf benefit we were a major sponsor of in June. I told her to bring another Hooters server, and I would get them gold shirts with our stucco company logo. She was instructed to wear golf-appropriate shorts. Rachel brought Felicia, and *that* is how I became such good friends with Felicia. We had a blast at the golf benefit. Rachel and Felicia would slather greasy thick sunscreen all over the legs, necks, and arms of the golfers. The men would say, "*You* don't work for that stucco company."

Rachel would smart off back. "Yes we do…Today we work for Bret."

As I walked Rachel and Felicia back to their car, I explained to Rachel that since she was twenty-four, I was perhaps too old for her. "You are not too old, Bret. I know that you are in your thirties, and that is okay," Rachel boasted.

"Rachel…I am in my thirties but only until the end of the summer," I explained.

"What does that mean?" Rachel asked.

Felicia chimed in, "He has a birthday late in the summer and turns forty." That is also how Felicia and I found out we share the same birthday in August. Small world.

"Well, I still don't care...I really like you Bret." Rachel grabbed me with a big hug around the waist, and I nearly fell on the asphalt parking lot.

Rachel and I spent a lot of time together that summer until when while we were goofing off at Victoria's Secret in the Coronado Mall, her girlfriend's sister spotted us and confronted Rachel. Long story short, the girlfriend found out, beat up Rachel, kicked her out of the house they rented, and Rachel made plans to move to Dallas where she was from originally. Rachel's friend Patty flew out so she could drive back to Dallas with Rachel. I did not have the opportunity to meet Patty at that time. I made Rachel a care basket with Powerbars, juice bottles, and candy for the drive back to Dallas.

Rachel and I remained friends, and she flew to Albuquerque for our golf benefit the very next year and stayed as my guest in my home for the weekend. I went to visit Rachel in Dallas on two separate occasions, where I would meet her best friend Patty a few months after *we* bailed Rachel out of jail. Each time Rachel would get me at Love Field in Dallas, she would wear a cute little form-fitting dress and would get the craziest enthusiastic smile when she would spot me in the crowd. Rachel was on the reality TV courtroom show *Eye for and Eye* hosted by Kato Kaelin and featuring Judge "Extreme Akim." It was cool watching her on TV knowing that Rachel was my friend and had been my house guest for a weekend and I had been her guest twice.

When Rachel graduated from a cosmetology school, she invited a bunch of people to attend her party. I flew out to Dallas for the event and stayed with Rachel at her apartment. We went to a cool night club with these big muscle-bound bouncer doormen in tight black t-shirts. Rachel was in a sweet cocktail dress, and I looked like a goober from New Mexico in a Lacoste polo shirt. I love those crocodile and khaki olive hiking shorts with hiking boots. I brought clothes, but Rachel took me directly to the club from the airport. The young people in Dallas were dressed super nice: the men in dress slacks with French cuffs and starched dress shirts with the sleeves rolled up, the ladies in dresses. It was summer, and we were outside by a swimming pool with laser beams and a light show. The movie *Zoolander* was displayed on the side of a tall building adjacent, and wild techno music was blasted so loud from the DJ booth.

There were beach balls floating in the pool, and Rachel suggested we get in the shallow end and bounce the balls to each other. We took off our shoes and entered the pool. Every so often a ball would bounce on top of the water and splash the "cool" crown of Dallas young people sipping vodka and Red Bull. Both men and women gave us dirty looks. Laughing, Rachel grabbed me tight with her arms around my neck. She went in for what I thought was a kiss, just like Elizabeth Hurley in the movie *Bedazzled* when she whispered into Brendan Frasier's ear, "I'm the devil."

With both of us standing in the shallow end of the pool, Rachel leaned next to me, touching her cheek on my cheek, and standing tiptoe since I am clearly a foot taller. Rachel said into my ear, "All the men here want to be *you* tonight."

Chapter Five
The Telemundo Woman

It was the dawn of the twenty-first century and I was working at Furr's once again as a manager, this go-around in Albuquerque. I had done a stint with Furr's in Denver starting in 1989, then in Arvada; Pueblo; and Boulder, Colorado, when I left the company for other opportunities in 1994. I had worked my way up from associate manager to general manager in short period of time. That BA in fine arts from The Colorado College in Colorado Springs required me to take a foreign language at the intermediate level. What they neglect to tell you is that one must first take the elementary level before arriving at the intermediate level. My faculty advisor told me to take French "because the French lady in that department will allow the art students to make up the class during the summer when they fail."

"When they fail?" Whatever…Since I always thought Mexican and Spanish women were so hot with their brown skin and jet-black hair like a panther, I took Spanish. I took four blocks in a row, and the classes were conducted in Spanish. Damn that was hard. The Colorado College only offers courses on the block plan. One class at a time. Each block is three-and-one-half weeks, and then a Thursday-to-Sunday block break. Kind of a joke with some classes, but Spanish...*ay caramba.* Hey...I graduated. Hence...*Eso es porque yo puedo hablar en Espanol...leer y escribir tambien.*

After college I spent about fifteen years as a restaurant manager... Spanish served me well.

YSC! You're So Cool!

Back to Furr's in Albuquerque. We were doing breakfast on Saturday and Sunday, and the shift was a dog since we had *no* customers in the morning. To drum up business for breakfast on the weekend, I would take fresh-baked pies, like cherry or pecan, to the area motels. I would thank the people at the front desk for sending *all* of those customers for breakfast at Furr's at Coors and Interstate 40 on Saturday and Sunday, and offer gratitude and appreciation with fresh, hot, right-out-of-the-oven pies. I told them *not* to cut into the pie right away because it was so fresh and hot. Long story short, it worked, and in a couple short weeks we had a couple hundred people from the motels in the area joining us for breakfast on Saturday and Sunday.

Since we experienced a boost in breakfast activity our general manager hired additional employees just for the shift. No one wants to go to work at 4:45 A.M., so it was not easy. One of the new hires was a fifteen or sixteen year-old young woman we called Banda. She was super pretty and looked just like the Mexican women on the tele-novelas or crazy variety shows on Telemundo. Hence, she became known as the Telemundo woman. At first I thought there was no way in hell she would be worth a shet since she was a young kid and the breakfast shift started at 4:45 A.M. on Saturday and Sunday. Banda boasted that *this* was her first ever job, and she became one of the very best employees in the entire Furr's Cafeteria.

Back in the day when we would hire an employee, paperwork was literally paperwork. The I-9 form for eligibility to work in the USA was a sheet of paper on which we handwrote in ink pen the information from an employee, like photo ID, Social Security Card, Resident Alien. Later at the end of each week we would mail our paperwork to the corporate office to review and file.

About three weeks after Banda the Telemundo woman started with us as our best employee in her first job ever, the Furr's Corp office phoned and said that her paperwork was screwy, and she had to be terminated immediately.

"Hey Banda." I tapped her on the shoulder as she was serving a customer on the serving line on a weekday afternoon. She had been such a great weekend breakfast employee that we gave her some late afternoon shifts after school.

"What is it?" she asked with her plump lips in a Spanish accent. She has informed all of us that she hailed from Monterrey in Nuevo Leon, Mexico.

I asked Banda to follow me to the time clock, so as not to broadcast to everyone that she needed to clock out now since the Furr's Corp Office said Uncle Sam could not permit Banda to legally work in the USA.

"Can I at least finish the day?" Banda the Telemundo woman said, stern and in control.

"No...sorry. You need to clock out right now," I answered.

With that, Banda departed, only to return the very next day with an all new ID...name and all.

"Sorry," I told Banda. "We cannot rehire you, especially the very next day with a new name and ID papers."

I felt so bad for the kid, but the law is the law.

Just a few months later I was promoted to general manager at the Furr's on Second Street right near the Big I…the creative and original name provided for the interchange where Interstate 25 and Interstate 40 cross and intersect. The Big I was going through a major two-year massive rip down and start all over again cluster fawk of biblical proportions. The Furr's on Second Street in Albuquerque "had" in the past been one of the highest volume cafeterias in the entire Furr's network. Now under my leadership, it was touch-and-go depending upon the scope and scale of construction on any given day.

Banda the Telemundo woman would often come in to see me since I was her very first boss. Banda would bring in other little Telemundo Mexican girls and always dressed nice. Once in a while I would buy them lunch. They were skinny young women and did not eat much, especially on Furr's all-you-can-eat standards. Banda would also visit alone and ask again and again if I could hire her to work for me.

"I have been in the US since I was five, Meestur Bret," she would tell me in her Spanish accent.

"Sorry Banda," I would answer. "We can get in trouble…serious trouble and even go to jail if we hire someone we know is illegal."

Banda would answer back with, "I can get good papers…No one would know."

I did not see Banda much until later when sites like Myspace and Facebook were all the rage on the internet. I found Banda and noticed that she was a single Mom of two boys and that her mother lived with her. We visited off and on with little frequency on the internet.

A decade into the twenty-first century during the final term of Obama, the only US president who will go down in history as the only US president to go down in US history, I made contact with Banda the Telemundo woman.

She was a property manager for apartments near the Albuquerque International Airport, and our big stucco company had just moved the office to the plant, also near the Albuquerque International Airport. Hence, I invited Banda to meet me for lunch at Quarters BBQ near the UNM Stadium and Isotopes Park.

I made Mark, one of my employees, come with me to meet Banda for lunch. She was just as pretty as ever with her plump pouty lips and light-toast skin with brown sandy hair. Lunch was as if we had never spent several years apart. Not sure why I thought Mark need to join us…Oh well.

YSC! You're So Cool!

Banda and I started meeting for lunch more often. We liked to meet at Ojos Locos near Louisiana and Interstate 40…kind of a Mexican-themed sports bar with little tacos and such on the menu. I would arrive early…because for some reason I am always ten to fifteen minutes early everywhere I go.

"When the Telemundo woman arrives, bring her to my table," I would tell the slender hostess at Ojos Locos.

The hostess would direct Banda to my table, and Banda would be wearing such amazing professional business clothes…slacks with a dress blouse, a pencil skirt, high heels.

"What did the hostess say when you arrived?" I would ask Banda.

"The hostess did not say anything," Banda would respond. "She just brought me right over to the table."

I would burst out laughing and say, "I told the hostess to bring the Telemundo woman to my table when she arrives."

Banda would always roll her eyes and say to me, "Yeah, whatever."

"Banda you are so pretty just like a Telemundo woman," I would continue. "When I tell the hostess to bring the Telemundo woman to my table, it is so obvious that it is you when you arrive."

We started having lunch at least once per week, or I would bring Subway or something to Banda in her office when she was too busy to get away and meet. She was working at a brand new apartment complex, which was partially under construction, and since I was driving around every day in the big nasty yellow H2 Hummer, I kind of enjoyed dropping off lunch to Banda. All of the construction workers would check her out...the well-dressed business attire, the Telemundo woman property manager.

It was actually our stucco being used on the complex.

One afternoon as I was at my desk in my swanky office...I do have a nice cattle baron/oil tycoon office...I was so surprised when I noticed a call from Banda on my smart phone. "Hello, this Bret how may we help you?" I said all crazy enthusiastic like an AM Radio personality.

Banda laughed and said, "Did you not see me on the caller ID Meestur Bret?" Her Spanish accent is so sexy.

"Sure I did," I laughed. "But I do my best to be consistent. What's up?"

"Well," Banda started. "INS was here, and all of your workers ran off up and down the different streets. The stucco mixer is still running. There are hard hats and lunch pails all over the place."

I burst out laughing like I did the very first time I watched the Mel Brooks movie *Blazing Saddles* scene where the cowboys were farting around the campfire. I had trouble maintaining my composure but was finally able to say, "Aw Banda...you're so sweet. We only make the stucco, then a distributor buys our stucco, and that distributor sells that stucco to an applicator."

"Okay," Banda said. "What should I do?"

"Sit tight and wait about ten to twenty minutes," I instructed Banda." Then call me back. If no one comes by, I will make some calls."

Like clockwork, Banda called me in about twenty minutes. "Bret... a big heavy man with silver glasses is here. He turned off the stucco mixer, and now he is gathering up all the hard hats and lunch pails."

"Sounds cool, Banda. Let me know tomorrow if anyone returns to work." I was still laughing.

It was after that day when Banda, now in her late twenties, informed me that she was still not legal to work in the USA despite living here since she was five years old.

"Damn Telemundo woman," I told Banda. "You better fix your situation. Obama is leaving the White House, and the next president, no matter Democrat or Republican, will make some changes."

One of my associates, Orlando, had come to the US when he was in high school with his family, and they all did the process, resident alien, permanent resident alien, citizenship. Orlando was the sales manager for L&P Supply, one of my top distributers and well as one of the top in the entire nation with the company I represented. Orlando had said that an immigration lawyer is a must in these situations, and the illegal person may be required to leave the US and apply at a US consulate or embassy in Mexico.

"I don't know, Bret," Orlando said. "When a couple is married, they leave them alone, and the process is faster."

Banda had mentioned that her older sister was married to a Puerto Rican and they had hired an immigration attorney...a nice white lady who spoke perfect Spanish with an office right down the street from the Barella's Coffee Shop near the National Hispanic Culture Center in the Albuquerque South Valley. Always up for James Bond intrigue and adventure, the wheels in my head began spinning for days.

Banda and I were enjoying a sandwich at a Subway location near the Expo NM State Fairgrounds on Central Avenue when I told her my plan.

"OK Banda, you own your mobile home outright and the property manager job actually requires you to live on site in an apartment...Correct?" I asked.

"Yes," Banda answered. "Since I do not want to live in one of the apartments rent-free, they let a maintenance man live there."

"Okay, Banda." I was getting nervous. "You and I have been spending a lot of time together...Lunch a couple times per week... dinner. What if you and I spoke to the same immigration lawyer as your sister and we set things straight with your situation?"

"Oh my God Bret! Are you serious? Don't joke about this..." Banda was nearly in tears.

"Yes, I am serious," I went on. "We have been spending so much time together. We need to do this right with the immigration lawyer. Do exactly what she says. You pay for all the fees required by the lawyer and the US government"

She started wrapping up her half-eaten Subway sandwich...I think it was grilled chicken breast with Habanero sauce and jalapenos. Banda rose from the table, wrapped her hand behind my neck, and pulled me close, and as I was still seated gave me a quick kiss, and she was off and out the door.

Banda arrived at my home later that evening in her silver and sad PT Cruiser with bashed in ass-end. We visited about the details and decided not to delay. She would need to tell her employer...and certainly lose her job. She had the money from what she had been saving. Banda had lived in the US for well over twenty years, since the age of five, and had been illegal all this time, but now was on the path to become a citizen.

When I waited for Banda outside to get our marriage license from the Bernalillo County Clerk, I was so super nervous until I watched Banda walk across Civic Center Plaza. She looked like Jennifer Lopez or some other sexy Latin pop star. She was in a nice, well-fitted dress and high heels. Such a Telemundo woman.

We were instructed by the immigration lawyer to have joint utility accounts as well as banking. I later phoned CenturyLink and informed them of my pending marriage, and they added Banda. The electric company did the same, over the phone and in minutes...so easy. I was beginning to wonder why illegal immigrants did nothing to change their situation.

I do not know what the lawyer charged, since Banda paid, but I think it was about six thousand dollars. We had agreed on just a civil ceremony with a judge at the Bernalillo County Courts in Albuquerque when Banda at the last minute wanted to have a ceremony with well-dressed people, friends, and her family. Oh fawk...A semi-real wedding.

I had on a coat and tie with my dress cowboy boots, and Banda was in a nice dress. When she arrived in her sad little PT Cruiser, the Mexicans kept coming out like a clown car in a circus. Other cars arrived...her mother and other family members. The ceremony was very brief and in Spanish.

Someone said, "Let's go to Gardunos!" and off we went to Gardunos Mexican Restaurant and Cantina outside of Win Rock Mall. (It's pronounced Gar– Dune-Yoes). The Mariachis played for us, and I had a Law of Attraction moment. I remembered watching that movie *Jerry Maguire* starring Tom Cruise on cable one night at my friend Bruce's home in Longmont, Colorado, and Mariachis played at the wedding of Jerry McGuire in that movie.

"The next time I get married," I told Bruce. "there will be Mariachis." Bruce always hosted big-ass BBQ cookouts, and his home was the hangout. There were about ten to fifteen people there, and they all laughed at me. Wonder what they would say if they could see my Telemundo bride now.

Everything was in order. Banda went and properly changed her name on her New Mexico driver's license. The next step would be to add Banda to one of my bank accounts. I have several bank and credit union accounts, and I chose the credit union where I had financed my

Hummer. Banda met me there late one afternoon so we could open an account with her. By now Banda had her US issued Social Security card and her resident alien card.

"Well, it's just not that easy, Sir. We cannot add your wife to your account," the woman from the credit union informed us.

"That makes absolutely *no* sense. " I added, "We are legally married, hired an immigration lawyer, and we are properly taking the legal steps. She has a Social Security card."

"Well, if only you had documents like a utility bill or a phone bill, then perhaps we could add your spouse to the account," The dry and stern bank officer told us.

"Oh, no problem," Banda sprang up out of her seat. "I have some bills out in the car." She returned with the CenturyLink and electric company bill receipts.

And with that, Banda was on my account, complete with checkbook and ATM card. I added her to one of my Visa cards with her name stamped on the card, and I added her to my company health insurance, dental, and vision. On one of the next times we had gone to dinner, Banda pulled out a sleek new pair of glasses so she could read the menu.

YSC ! You're So Cool!

"Hey Banda!" I yelled one day. "What is your dream car?"

"My dream car…" Banda was puzzled. "What?"

"If you could have any car," I continued, "what would you drive?"

"Oh, a Nissan Murano," Banda smartly replied.

"A Nissan what? MooRanew?" I sarcastically said. "What the hell is that?"

"It's a cute crossover SUV," Banda defended her selection. "It is a cool little car."

"Why not a Nissan Xtera?" I asked. "If I get you a car, I want to get something I want to drive."

"Nope, Nissan Murano," Banda continued to respond proudly. "*That* is my dream car, and *you* asked."

"Oh, I know...How about a Range Rover?" I asked seriously, "The women on the Mexican telenovelas on Telemundo always drive Range Rovers."

"Do *you* have Range Rover money?" Banda defiantly asked.

"Hey I just paid off my H2 Hummer," I said, now getting hot under the collar. "I can certainly afford a Range Rover."

Banda was dead set on a Nissan Murano even though I begged and pleaded about a Range Rover purchase. Banda the Telemundo woman and I made a deal. I would purchase her dream car and place both of our names on the title, registration, and insurance, and Banda would make the monthly payments.

I made the purchase from Gary at Houston Wholesalers in Albuquerque. They specialize in late model, low-mile vehicles...generally Lexus, Mercedes, Audi...and Range Rover. Gary just happened to have a sweet little black Nissan Murano. I made the purchase on my Saturday day off and told Banda to get the hell over to my house right after she was done with work that afternoon...and ask a friend to drive.

"I didn't doubt you," Banda said as I handed her the key FOB, "but it seemed too good to be true." She and her friend raced up to the outlets in Santa Fe, where Banda purchased a new Coach bag.

In New Mexico a lot of women have Coach bags, just like a lot of men wear Ralph Lauren clothes. Remember the character Alan on the hit CBS TV show *Two and a Half Men*? The clothes worn by Alan are what is generally available at the Ralph Lauren Store in the Santa Fe Outlets. I like to wear plain white Oxfords or small pinstripe Oxfords from the Ralph Lauren brand for work and Lacoste polo shirts for my time off...I love that crocodile...I have observed at Santa Fe Area Home Builder Association Board meetings that some ladies would wear a dress with the Ralph Lauren logo while men would either be in a Ralph Lauren logo t-shirt, a polo shirt, Oxford dress shirt, or three-quarter zip sweater...Oh, yeah, I daydream and people watch a lot...an awful lot.

About a week later Banda received the news that since she was married to Bret, she no longer qualified for some sort of government assistance which provided milk for her young boys. "Damn, Banda," I laughed. "How much milk do they drink? If you can't get milk, I will buy it from the store."

"It just doesn't seem fair," Banda said.

"Hey," I said, still laughing, "you are driving around in a near-new Nissan Moo Randeau...whatever...and you have a *new* Coach Bag. The days of government handouts are over."

"Yeah, I guess you're right," Banda said as she looked at me and smiled.

"That's why people think poorly of Mexicans," I told Banda. "True, there are a lot of government handouts and free stuff...but does that make it right to take advantage and assume you are entitled to a share?"

The Xmas season with Banda was so cool. Her Mexican family purchased a super nice Kenneth Cole dark-grey dress coat. I guess since they always noticed me in a black police-style jacket with my company logo, they thought I did not own a coat. The tamales Banda's mom made were so crazy out of this world...I could inhale those things.

The Puerto Rican married to Banda's sister, Roberto, was a culinary academy graduate chef who was always the head chef at a hotel or one of the area casinos in Albuquerque. On Sunday, Banda's sister's home was always the big hangout. We would have ribeye steaks on the grill...shrimp...Oh man...lots of incredible food. Roberto and Patty, Banda's sister, would host dinner parties in their home nearly every weekend. Patty was impressed when I knew who Frida, the famous Mexican painter was, after I noticed her portrait on the living room wall. One can know all about Benito Juarez, Pancho Villa, and more, but if you really want to make serious points with Mexicans... especially Mexican women, you better know all about Frida. I suggest watching the movie about Frida starring Selma Hayek.

I would go with Banda to watch her boys play soccer and even pick them up from school when she was busy. Big Surge and Handsome Dave is what I called those boys, and we even played putt-putt mini golf on San Mateo and went to Hinkle Family Fun Center to crash into each other on the bumper cars.

It was a real kick being married to Banda the Telemundo woman and a lot of fun while it lasted.

When we decided to split up and move on after she became a permanent resident alien and well on her way to full US citizenship, we met at the courthouse to file for our non-contested divorce. Standing in line with Banda, she looked up at me and said, "I want the Hummer."

In a cool, calm George Clooney voice I said, "That old ugly yellow thing. It's parked across the street at Wells Fargo if you are serious."

After the clerk handed us both copies of the divorce papers, I gave Banda and her mother both a hug and told her, "Don't be a stranger, and keep in touch."

Over the years Banda has kept in touch, and I often sponsor the soccer teams of Big Surge and Handsome Dave. Banda now drives a cool Caddy SUV of some sort...black and elegant.

Banda told me once, "You saved my life, Bret."

Chapter Six
Invite Her to do Laundry in Your Home

I had worked for just a little more than a year with the big stucco company and had learned a lot from everyone. Dave, the oldest of our team, during my training would always introduce me as, "The guy who will be running the outfit someday, and Bret will be our boss."

We were in the process of merging with a couple other large stucco companies, and we had corporate visitors in Albuquerque often arriving from Atlanta, Georgia, or Anaheim, California. Our sales director Richard would instruct me to pick up people from the Albuquerque Airport and bring them back to the corporate office or the plant. The National Director of Marketing, Duane, was in Albuquerque with a photographer to get shots of high-profile projects, when I had the duty to drive them around in my '95 Chevy Tahoe. Those days were so much fun! I had been asked to move to Anaheim and work with marketing at the National Corporate Offices. Each time I declined the offer, so I could remain in my humble Albuquerque home.

My uncle in Colorado had suddenly passed away, and I requested a couple vacation days from Richard our sales director. My uncle was only sixty and the older and only brother to my mom. Since my dad worked in the oil field/petroleum industry, the long hours required kept him away at work. Hence, my uncle was always around for school events and even Cub Scout meetings. It should be noted that when I was young, the Cub Scouts were all the rage, and it was so cool to wear that uniform to elementary school. I wanted the uniform because the blue shirt and yellow scarf looked like the US Cavalry in those old John Wayne movies. My mom never let me play John Wayne in my Cub Scout uniform.

Anyway, my son was eleven years old at the time and on spring break, so I dragged him away from my ex-wife for the trip to Colorado. My daughter was in San Diego with one of her school buddies, so she did not make the trip. It would be a ten to twelve hour drive from Albuquerque, New Mexico to my hometown of Sterling, Colorado, and my son Mac was up for a road trip, despite knowing there would be a funeral once we reached our destination.

"Can I run inside and get some chips, Dad?" Mac asked me as I pumped gas in Rocky Ford, Colorado. I gave him some cash and sent him inside. A few miles down the two-lane highway (I bypass Denver and the big front-range cities) we were headed north in the very flat eastern plains of Colorado. Mac was crunching away on chile picante Corn Nuts, and I swore he was going to break a tooth. He offered some of the hard-as-rock Corn Nuts with hot chile picante dust, and I crunched and sucked until I could not stand it...My lips were on fire.

"Did You get us a Coke or anything to drink?" I asked with tears in my eyes.

"Nope," Mac laughed. "Just these chips." (People from New Mexico call nearly *all* snack foods in a bag "chips," and virtually any soft drink no matter what is referred to as a coke.)

When we arrived in Sterling, it was only around 2:30 P.M., and we had made record time. It was a hot, sunny, beautiful spring day. Since we had time to burn, I took Mac to the campus of Northeastern

Junior College, where I spent my freshman and sophomore years before transferring to The Colorado College in Colorado Springs to complete my BA in Fine Arts. Northeastern has a small campus but has several large dormitories, classroom buildings, athletic facilities, and a sweet student center. Many of the buildings are in a mid-century, modern style since they were built in the late fifties and early sixties of the twentieth century. There are a lot of basketball players and other athletes attending Northeastern in an effort to better their academic grades and fine tune their athletic abilities so they can transfer to a big university.

As Mac and I were walking around, a large group of students loudly came running out of the main doors of the student center. One of the young women was African American and super attractive in a polo shirt and tiny Khaki shorts. I have a thesaurus next to me as I write, but let's just say she could have been a Victoria's Secret model or a movie star...

"Mmm," I said out loud. "I need someone like her."

"Who?" asked my eleven-year-old son Mac.

"That tiny girl in the shorts," I said, pointing.

My son rolled his eyes and said, "Whatever. . . ."

YSC ! You're So Cool ! Be careful what YOU wish for,…

Fast forward to just after Thanksgiving in November of the same year. Our office manager, Lola, had just hired a new receptionist for our office, and she was taking the young lady around on a tour of the place and to meet everyone. I noticed Lola with the new hire in the mailroom and I took advantage to introduce myself.

There she was...*No*, not exactly the same young woman, but Rajah, the new hire Lola brought in to fill our vacant receptionist position, was standing before me. Yes, Rajah looked like a Victoria's Secret model…smile, body, eyes…crazy curly flowing hair, nails. Rajah had just completed working at Forever 21 in the Coronado mall, so she had some super nice dress clothes. I have come to find that those jobs pay a suitable commission to young ladies working there, but the real advantage is the employee discount used to build a great wardrobe.

As we stood in the mailroom, Lola, Rajah, and me making pleasant conversation and salutations, the phone rang, and Rajah excused herself so she could get up to the cool reception desk at the front lobby area and take the call.

"What's the story on this new girl Lola?" I asked.

"She turns twenty next week and hands off…She has a boyfriend," Lola answered, stern and serious.

Lola and most of the office staff departed each day at 4:30 P.M. Our sales director, Richard, had scheduled me to spend afternoons from three to five available to answer phones in the event of technical calls or if someone arrived at the corporate office for stucco samples and the like. Rajah was also scheduled to work until 5:00 P.M.

Richard would typically work in the late afternoon, meeting with Kenney our CFO in his office at the back of our building. There were four ladies who did accounting back there as well as Mr. Miley, out IT guy.

I was stuck with Rajah late in the afternoons, right up to 5:00 P.M. She was super smart and had wanted to attend school to be a veterinary assistant, since she was an animal lover. She lived alone in a studio apartment while her mom and dad traveled around the country as over-the-road team truck drivers. Rajah's parents were seldom ever in Albuquerque. She had two older brothers.

Rajah and I had limited contact during the daytime office hours and only visited briefly when we were alone before 5:00 P.M. each day. Other than a simple hello exchanged as I entered the building or simple banter as Rajah delivered mail to my desk, it was for the most part just business and professional.

Rajah had been with us for about a full month, and she was really working out, when our architect rep. Andy called me. "Dude, you need to get back to the office."

"Relax," I answered on my cell phone as I was driving around a residential construction site in Rio Rancho just northwest of Albuquerque. Back then, single homes were being built by the thousands and over the horizon with—you guessed it—stucco we manufactured. "I am scheduled to return at 3:00 P.M. for office duty."

"Well Rajah has been in the bathroom all day crying because she had some sort of fight with her boyfriend," Andy chimed in. "Lola wants to send her home, but Rajah says she lives alone and needs the hours for rent money."

As I entered the front door, Rajah had clearly been crying, but she maintained a professional appearance and composure. I avoided eye contact and just said, "Hey Raj, any messages for me or mail?"

"No Bret," Rajah said.

When Andy, Lola, and most of the other staff departed for the day at 4:30 P.M., I left my desk and went up to the cool receptionist desk in our lobby to visit with Rajah.

As I handed Rajah my business card, I said, "My cell number is on here, but you already know that number. I wrote my home number down too. It sounds like you had a rough day today, and we do not need to get into that right now. Just call me later if you want to talk."

"Okay," was all that Rajah whispered. We said nothing at 5:00 P.M. when we both got in our cars in the parking lot, going home in different directions.

A couple weeks later I attended a Remodelor's Council lunch monthly meeting. These functions usually took place in a shop or warehouse of a business and often were a box lunch with sandwiches, an apple, a cookie, and a bag of chips. I saved my bag of chips, and as I returned to our corporate office that day, I tossed the bag on Rajah's desk and said, "Hey Rajah, *you* are all that and a bag of chips."

Rajah laughed out loud and said, "Thanks!"

Lola said, "I swear, Bret…You better not be bothering her."

Rajah laughed again.

That very Saturday morning, after visiting with my mom at 6:00 A.M. on the phone as always, I was doing laundry and cleaning my house waiting for the call or text from Felicia at Hooters inviting me to join her on the patio for lunch. The washer and dryer were running loudly, and I had the vacuum going all over. I am super bad about my house. I constantly get accused of having a cleaning lady. Nope, I just have OCD really, bad and I clean, and clean, and clean again, with Saturday as the monumental day of cleaning activity.

I noticed the red light blinking on the old-school twentieth-century digital answering machine next to my landline phone in the master bedroom. Hmm…most everyone calls my cell phone.

"Hi Bret, this is Rajah," she started on her digital message, sounding confident. "I hope it is okay to call your home phone. I was wondering if you would like to meet at Century Rio and catch a movie tonight since it is Saturday. I know you said you wanted to see *The Aviator* with Leonardo DiCaprio, but I want to see that *Oceans* movie with George Clooney. I hope it's okay to ask. Call me back," Rajah continued, now sounding nervous and talking a mile per minute.

During lunch that day at Hooters, I was so crazy happy and in a great mood. "Felicia!" I started. "Rajah from work called me and asked *me* to meet *her* at the movies."

"Yeah, so you said that you gave her your number, didn't you buddy?" Felicia smarted back at me in her Hooters uniform. "Did you call her back? Don't make her wait."

Rajah was wearing this fuzzy light-purple sweater showing off her Victoria's Secret model figure when we met in the lobby at the Century Rio movies that night. Wow, I could not believe I was going to the movies with such an attractive young woman...just like the women I had noticed months earlier at Northeastern Junior College when I smarted off to my son, "I want a woman like her."

Not one to argue, I went with Rajah's suggestion, and we watched the George Clooney movie. There was a light and cold drizzle of rain in the parking lot when she hugged me super tight around my ribs. Her perfume was to die for.

I played it cool on Monday when we returned to work. I told Rajah that it was okay as coworkers to spend time together outside of work but that we should be discrete and not the center of attention and gossip. Rajah agreed, and we began to go to dinner and spend a lot of time together.

"Do You save up quarters, or do you get like a roll of quarters at a store or bank when it's time for laundry?" I asked Rajah. "Is there a laundry room at your apartment or do you go off site?"

"Yeah, laundry sucks all right," was the reply from Rajah.

"Well," I began. 'I am just throwing this out there. If you want, just bring your laundry to my place and I can teach You how to make margaritas and maybe even shrimp pasta alfredo while you do your laundry."

Rajah was so happy with the idea that she arrived at my home that very night. As she was removing laundry from the basket she brought, her shirt hiked up her back and I could not help but notice she was wearing thong panties...OMG! Be careful what you wish for.

Since I have all the cool bar stuff, cocktail shakers, margarita glasses, wine goblets, champagne flutes and the like, Rajah thought she had been cast in an old Dean Martin movie. I used my good dishes and cloth napkins for dinner that night. As a restaurant manager for fifteen years after college, I can whip out some great food. I do not mean to brag…but aw fawk, I will brag when there is an opportunity. I can cook anything, and I am an amazing cook.

Soon Rajah would make margaritas, and I would sit back, and she would serve me using all of the cool bar stuff in my home. Having dinner at my place became a regular event, and soon we hardly ever visited a Chinese buffet again. Rajah mentioned that since I lived so far on the westside, would I mind coming for her after work and then driving her to my place? Duh…no problem. Rajah also had a tiny chihuahua puppy she named Bo just like Paris Hilton, and soon Bo would join us for dinner each evening.

The weekends were the best. I would make Italian, and we would share a bottle of wine. Rajah would bring Tyson hot chicken breast strips so she could make dinner for me. At work we still kept everything a secret.

"Rajah, did you do anything fun this weekend?" Lola asked one Monday morning as we were in the employee breakroom wiping out a box of messy Krispy Crème donuts Dave had brought.

"Yeah," Rajah answered. "I kind of started seeing this guy. He is older and makes me dinner at his home. He taught me how to make margaritas…He has all kinds of cool bar stuff."

"Aw Rajah, that is so nice," Lola tilted her head and said," I am glad you are having fun."

I was making a mess and getting chocolate all over my face. "Damn I love all things chocolate."

Rajah burst out laughing at me, and she made eye contact with Lola.

Lola looked at me. "And you, Bret. Did you have fun this weekend?"

"Oh hell yeah," I said as I polished off a nasty chocolate Krispy Crème. "I have been spending a lot of time with this woman, making dinner for her in my home."

"Good for *you!*" Lola said. "Good for both of *you*…That's so nice. I am glad you both have found people."

Rajah and I looked at each other and laughed so hard. Sometimes it is best to hide in plain sight, and no one will ever notice.

I had a key to my place made for Rajah and had a key ring from Things Remembered with "Dark Little Secret" engraved with fancy script. She thought it was so cool. When I traveled out of town, like to El Paso or Colorado Springs, Rajah would stay at my home with her friend Lilianna. I never met Lilianna, and to this day I do not even know what she looks like. I can recall purchasing Jose Cuervo, pudding, hot Cheetos, and Tyson hot chicken strips from Smith's Supermarket for Rajah to stock up on at my home when I would travel, and the cashier would say, "Boy, this looks like a party I would like to attend."

Valentines was fast approaching and no one at work even knew that Rajah was with me at my house all weekend and several nights during the week. I told Rajah that we could get a big pizza from Dion's and just hang out. She was fine with that, and she said that since I liked Fergie, the singer from The Black Eyed Peas, Rajah would wear some sort of sexy crop top to show off her abs and look sexy for me.

Little did Rajah know that I had some panties from Victoria's Secret complete with the ever-popular Victoria's Secret gift bag and pink paper with a sweet Snoopy Valentine Card. I also went to Walmart, where I did a do-it-yourself flower arrangement combining two different sets of red and white roses. Remember, I possess a BA degree in Fine Arts from The Colorado College. The flowers did not even cost much since the Walmart cashier merely scanned the tag on the bottom of the vase...Bang! I did not even intend for that to happen.

I picked up Rajah at her apartment after work, and oh *yes*...She was in such a cute crop top a la Fergie from The Black Eyed Peas. We called in our pizza to Dion's at Montano and Coors, where we went through the ever-popular Dion's call-in order drive-through window. When in Albuquerque, one must have Dion's damn good pizza, and it served the purpose that particular Valentine's with Rajah.

As I fumbled with the Dion's pizza, Rajah, holding her chihuahua Bo, entered my living room to see an arrangement of roses for a movie star, as well as the Victoria's Secret bag.

"Bret, you are like the men in the movies." Rajah said. "This is so unreal. You make me feel so special."

Rajah and I continued to spend a great deal of time together, having dinner at my home and out once at an Italian Restaurant.

"Will You share a bottle of wine with me tonight?" I asked Rajah as we waited for the hostess.

"Yeah right," Rajah rolled her eyes. "They will not serve me."

"Challenge accepted," I boldly said. "Watch this."

The hostess sat us at a table for two in a private area away from other tables with a young twenty-something male server.

"May we have a bottle of just the simple house Merlot please?" I asked. "My little girlfriend and I would enjoy some Merlot with dinner. You will share a bottle of Merlot with me, right? Yes, we will have Merlot with our meal tonight." Rajah just smiled and shook her head in the universal up-and-down motion to imply yes.

Looking at me and then the young Rajah with her jet-black curls cascading around her chocolate brown face and deep dark eyes, the server said, "Of course, Sir."

Upon his return, the server displayed a bottle of Merlot. Reading the label on the bottle, I shook my head in the universal up-and-down motion to imply yes, and the cork was popped. A tiny amount was splashed into my glass by the server, and I looked at the fermented grape beverage that for the history of man has opened so many doors with women. I sniffed the glass and then a tiny sip of the bitter warm hooch.

"Yes," I said, pleased. "This will do fine." And with that the server poured more Merlot into my glass and a glass for Rajah.

It was these *fun* and yet simple little moments that impressed

Rajah and compelled her to continue to spend so much quality time with me.

I would have In Bloom Flowers near the big stucco company corporate office deliver flowers...incredible white-and-red rose arrangements to Rajah and surprise the shit out of her. Lola our office manager at this point still had *no* clue that it was Bret whom Rajah would mention spending so much time with and having dinner with at his place...and receiving crazy flower arrangements on a whim and surprise.

Then...I went in for the kill. A surprise Victoria's Secret haul... bra, panties...Yum, five panties for a certain price and a special silk bra and panty set. Rajah shit a brick with sharp corner when the FedEx package arrived at the receptionist desk of the big stucco company corporate office and...it was for Rajah!

YSC ! You're So Cool.

I was walking up to the front door one afternoon with my arms full, boxes of samples from our lab located at the plant. Rajah ran and opened the door for me. Later, Janet from Accounts Receivables came over to my desk and mentioned how she noticed Rajah's door-opening actions.

"I think that little Rajah likes *you* Bret," Janet said with a smirk. Janet was older than me, mature, and knew the ways of the world.

"Naw," I said. "Rajah just noticed my arms were full."

"Yeah, right. I have never seen one of our girls jump and open a door for any of you sales guys like that before." Janet laughed and went back to her area.

On one particular Saturday Rajah had spent the night with me at my home. In the middle of the night as she was in the bathroom, I heard a little puppy growl from Bo, her tiny chihuahua. The miniature dog was attempting to sleep on one of my very expensive Lacoste polo shirts on the floor next to the bed. Mmm…I love that Lacoste crocodile.

"You little shit," I said to the chihuahua as he perked up with big brown wet eyes and a tail wagging so fast one would expect him to take off like a tiny helicopter. "That Lacoste cost me more than these sheets on this bed." With that, I scooped up Bo the tiny chihuahua and held him like a Teddy Bear as he licked my face.

"Aw…" Rajah said in excitement, wearing one of my plain crisp with t-shirts covering her petite frame like a dress. "That is so sweet, Bret. You are so nice to my dog. *You* have *no* idea the serious points *you* are making with me right now."

Later that week at work, Lola was wandering around the office saying out loud, "I have a secret…I have a *big* secret."

I blew it off and was confident that there was no way Rajah would have said anything to Lola.

Okay…get ready, sit up straight, and pay attention.

Rajah and I were in bed and she was twirling her nicely manicured fingers in my tangle of chest hair.

"I have something to tell you, Bret." Rajah looked up at me, raising her head.

"Yes," was all I could get out.

"Don't be mad, okay, " Rajah started. "I told Lola everything, and she is such a cool boss with me. She supports you and I together like this."

"Oh Rajah, we need to still be discreet so as not to draw attention and gossip." I said, calm and cool like George Clooney as I kissed her forehead. I am so *big* on the forehead kiss. The forehead is the mind's eye, or also known as the third eye. It is a big deal to kiss the forehead of a woman. Marilyn Monroe said, "The real lover is the man who can thrill you by kissing your forehead."

"You make me feel so special Bret," Rajah said. "I am not even a real woman yet. I am just a kid still."

"Whoa," I said. "It is because *you* are a real woman that I make dinner for you and let *you* spend the night with me and hang around and stuff."

As is the case with most at-work/office romances, word got out. Soon everyone knew that Rajah had keys to Bret's house and that she did far more than just laundry there.

In a moment of drama one afternoon, without saying a word, Rajah walked up to my desk and tossed my house key at me. She then walked away. We went a couple weeks without talking and soon there was a new and younger guy in her life dropping her off at work and then picking her up at 5:00 P.M. Oh, and she tossed the house key at me…only the house key. She kept the Things Remembered "Dark Little Secret" key ring.

I had a lot of stupid questions after that.

"How did this all start?" asked Richard our sales director. "You two okay to work together up until 5:00 P.M. in the office each day?"

"You? You and Rajah?" asked Marcos. "No way."

"How did she look naked?" asked Andy and Karl in unison.

"Really?" I answered. "Just like a Victoria's Secret model or a Playboy centerfold."

"Did she have a little black patch of Velcro?" asked Andy.

"I have not noticed pubic hair on a woman in person or otherwise since at least 1995." I answered, "I am not much for details, as it is bad luck to tell."

YSC ! You're So Cool!

Quite some time later, I had arrangements for a quick morning trip to Santa Fe to drop off a stucco sample to a distributor, and then I had requested the afternoon off so that I could attend an Albuquerque Isotopes semi-pro baseball game. The Isotopes are popular, and the games have super good attendance in a mid-century modern stadium known as the "Lab." The Isotopes were the farm team for the Marlins that year, I think…maybe the Dodgers. Not important, since I had seats right next to the dugout and third base on the wall.

On the drive back from Santa Fe I called the office with my cell as I was careening down Interstate-25 like a Monaco Grand Prix driver. Rajah, performing her prescribed duties, answered the phone.

"Yes!" I yelled into the phone.

"Bret, is that You?" Rajah spoke, "Is everything okay?"

I got into George-Clooney-calm character, "Rajah…tell Lola you have a stomach ache and meet me at your apartment at 11:30 so I can take you with me to the Isotopes businessman lunch game today. First pitch at noon sharp."

"No Bret," Rajah was stern and serious. "I am not going to tell Lola that I have a stomachache, and I am *not* going to a baseball game with *you*. I don't even like baseball."

"Rajah," I started, still in control, calm and cool like George Clooney. "It's not about the baseball. It's about cold beer, Blake's Lot A Burger, or Dion's Pizza and hanging out for an afternoon with someone you love."

"I do not love *you*, Bret." Rajah was so stern and serious. "I am not telling Lola I have a stomachache, and I am not meeting you at my house at 11:30."

I was rapidly approaching Bernalillo, and Albuquerque was next heading south on Interstate-25. I slowed down. "Rajah, I know that you love me and you want to go to this Isotopes game with me." I was still in character as George Clooney. I could picture the actor in my head. "Now put me on hold and go tell Lola that you have a stomachache and need to go home right now."

"Okay." Rajah placed me on hold, and I listened to bad music elevator music and a commercial about stucco.

"Okay…11:30?" asked Rajah.

"Yes Baby," I answered, still Clooney Cool, "and wear something cool. It's going to be a *hot* day."

Rajah had a powder-blue bandeau tube top and matching teeny-tiny shorts. Her jet-black crazy hair curls went up and then down to frame her chocolate face and smile. Her tan chocolate skin was so sexy she looked like a movie star. She had never attended an Isotopes game. She purchased a cute Isotopes sun visor from a vendor near the gate, and we started with ice-cold beer in our up front seats. It was not long before Orbit, the big orange fuzzy Isotopes mascot, would run up to the wall on the field side and hug Rajah as she would lean over the wall from our seats. The men in yellow security jackets said and did nothing. The Bueno Chile sponsor red and green chile mascots in their big foam chile costumes would also come over and hug Rajah. A giant soft tortilla foam taco as well would cop a feel and reach up from the field and hug Rajah. My guess is that all of these foam-clad "mascots," Orbit, Red Chile, Green Chile, and the White Soft Tortilla Taco, were all horny young guys.

Rajah was displayed on the scoreboard jumbotron numerous times, big smile and hugs from the "mascots."

"Man, Rajah. That is all we need for a builder or distributor of our stucco to see you up on the jumbotron after you told Lola that a stomach ache would send you home…not an Isotopes businessman lunch with Bret."

The day was super-hot in the sun, and the cold beer was flowing. I did not eat and neither did Rajah. The concessions are supreme at Isotopes Park, but we told ourselves that we would get Chinese buffet after the game. It has been way too many years now, but I do not know why in the hell Chinese buffet sounded like a good idea after attending a late summer afternoon Isotopes game with cold beer flowing.

Our seats, as previously stated, were right in the front row by the dugout and third base with virtually no one else around for several rows. In the bottom of the sixth inning, I noticed a man a few rows up holding a clear plastic cup with the Jose Cuervo logo and a lime wedge on the rim.

"Is that a margarita, Sir?" I asked. "Where can one get one of those?"

The man pointed and did not speak. I noticed a Jose Cuervo margarita vendor.

"Whoa Rajah," I said, excited. "Chug your beer, and we can switch to 'ritas before last call and the end of this game." It seemed like a good idea…We were having so much fun. I returned to the seats with a Jose Cuervo logo plastic cup, complete with lime wedge on the rim, and a cold sweet 'rita on the inside. Rajah was on her cell phone.

"Tron keeps hugging me, and I am having such a fawking good time here with Bret…He is always such a fawking blast. He is so dope!" Rajah was yelling into her phone over the baseball game crowd noise. "Okay…I will…see You tomorrow." She ended the call and wiped some loose jet-black curls of hair away from her sleepy-looking eyes, making direct contact with me and smiling.

"The screen is Tron, and *that* is Orbit." I said pointing with my finger at the Isotopes mascot as I handed the cool, sweet 'rita in Rajah's sexy manicured hands. "Who were you on the phone with just now."

Rajah took a deep, long gulp of her 'rita, sighed, and exclaimed, "Aw, I called Lola…I'm having such a fucking blast with you, Bret, that I thought Lola should know that I do not have a stomachache."

"Aw fuck, Rajah!" I was far from Clooney Cool now— more like Vince Vaughn. "Lola does not need to know. Besides, you just may have a killer stomachache tomorrow and miss work for sure."

When the game ended and a small tractor began to service the infield as other maintenance people started to clean the field and seats, Rajah went into the ladies room for what seemed like a college semester's length of time.

"Hey dude." Two chubby nerds approached me. "We decided your girlfriend was the hottest woman at the game today."

I did not answer but opted for the head tilt that would acknowledge that I was either too drunk to recall who I attended the game with or that I would certainly agree with the nerds. They both had round bellies as if they had never performed much exercise or certainly never a sit up or crunch.

They came closer, as if to become friends. "Where did *you* find her? She is beautiful."

I was able to recall the George Clooney calm character again. "Maybe she found me."

They both looked disappointed, and as I ignored them, I asked a female staff/janitor, "Can you go in the ladies room and check on my girlfriend? She has been in there a very long time."

The staff/janitor continued to sweep up popcorn and the general crap found after a sports event or tornado. "We don't do that," was her reply.

"Fine, I will go in and get her myself," I boasted. "Gentlemen, please excuse me," I said to the plump-bellied nerd boys as I entered the ladies room and my echo bounced off the walls. "Rajah, you okay?"

Rajah only weighed about a hundred pounds, and I just carried her like a kid across the street to the parking lot, where my '95 Tahoe was all alone, since everyone was long gone. After all that booze, I really should have never driven to Rajah's apartment. I can recall Bo the tiny chihuahua licking my face as I lay on the carpet and looked at the enormous tropical fish tank in Rajah's studio apartment. It felt like the room was spinning, and I grabbed onto the carpet to stable my body.

Rajah lay beside me and let out a deep breath sigh. "Not sure we should go to the Chinese buffet...I have a stomachache."

"I know you have a stomachache Rajah, "I laughed. "That's why Lola gave you the afternoon off."

"Stop! "Rajah laughed. "It's not funny...*You* got me all fucked up at the game."

"I told *you* to get a slice of Dion's Pizza or a Blake's Lot A Burger," I answered. "No one forced you to booze it up in the hot sun all day."

Rajah was laughing so hard I started to squeeze her hip and tickle her tight-toned tummy. Rajah began to twist and turn on the floor as if she were in a Grand Mal seizure. Suddenly one of Rajah's perfectly round, firm, young chocolate brown boobs popped out of the bandeau tube top, and we both laughed hard as she struggled to hide the big round globe. Suddenly I wanted a Reese's Peanut Butter Cup.

Rajah became serious and said, "We should not be doing this. Lay here until you're sober and then you need to go home Bret."

The next day Rajah looked green, and she was clearly not feeling well. Lola was mad at me, and Janet asked me about the stomachache Rajah had the day before. "Did you take her some soup and help her with convalescent activity?"

"No...not quite soup," I replied.

Rajah and I would smirk, smile, and become much more civil after the Isotopes game. However, Rajah also became far more serious with her new boyfriend. That was about the time I met Rachel at Hooters.

Rajah would become pregnant with her boyfriend, they would marry, and she would quit her job with us at the start of her pregnancy.

Women are much like cats. When we chase them...they run away. When we do our own thing and allow cats to do their own thing, the cat will often seek us out and jump on our lap as we try to read a book or watch TV. The cat will rub its head on us and purr. Never force relationships with women. We are far from dominant over women. Treat them as astute individuals and you just might experience great adventures and the like.

Are you ready for this? Pay attention. Here it comes...

A little more than a year later, Lola hired Rajah back in the same receptionist position. Rajah and I got along well and were professional.

"What are you doing for lunch? Meeting a client or can you take little old me?" Rajah called one day on my cell. And then it started.

Rajah and I began to have lunch often. I would tell her that I would pick her up or we would walk out the office door together right up to my '95 Tahoe and go to lunch. Hide in plain sight. No sneaking around. People notice you when there is sneaking around.

When I purchased the big nasty yellow H2 Hummer in July, the dealer delivered the beast to our office. Rajah was impressed with my new vehicle and the way the dealer delivered said yellow beast to my office. Rajah and I once again went to lunch, and when I brought her back to the office, I stopped in front with the motor running because I had an appointment with a client. As Rajah jumped out of her seat, her pencil shirt hiked up, and her blouse became untucked. As she shifted her pencil skirt and tucked in her blouse in front of the big stucco company corporate office, I said, "Rajah, please, do that in the ladies room not here outside for all to see."

Late one afternoon as I sat at my desk and Rajah was up front at her receptionist desk, my phone made the ever popular "ding" notification to signal I had received a text message. It was from Rajah, and the text read, "Meet me at Hooters for a beer after work?"

Roxy and Felicia were working the bar on the patio, and Rajah and I sat and talked. I kept drinking non-alcoholic beer because I was on a health kick and did not want to call Lola again for a ride to my home after drinking too much at Hooters, especially since I was with Rajah.

"Are you trying to get that little black girl drunk Bret?" Roxy asked. "Why are you drinking O'Doul's?"

Rajah was in the ladies room, and Felicia explained to Roxy, "Bret and that little black girl used to spend a lot of time together Rox."

When Rajah returned, I looked into her eyes and asked, "Would you like to go back to my place?"

Rajah shrugged her shoulders as I looked at my watch and noticed it was after 9:00 P.M. "What do you tell your mother-in-law when you and I meet after work like this?" I knew that Rajah lived with her mother-in-law, and the mother in law was her convenient, free baby-sitter/nanny.

"I tell the family that I have to work late." Rajah answered.

"What if they drive by the office and see it dark after 5:00 P.M.?" I asked.

Again Rajah only shrugged her shoulders with no verbal response.

"Rajah," I began. "Where is your husband?"

"Out of town," she answered abruptly.

"Well, it may not be a good idea to go to my house tonight," I suggested.

YSC ! You're So Cool!

Often Janet from Accounts Receivable would host dinner parties or just have people over to her big-ass mansion in Placitas, north of Albuquerque. Janet was married to Steve, who with his brother was part-owner of a large landscaping company. "Do you have plans for dinner tonight? I am making lasagna."

"I would love to come for dinner, Janet," I enthusiastically replied. "May I bring a date?"

"Of course," Janet smiled. "I had no idea you were even seeing anyone. Come by at about 7:00 *P.M.*"

I made arrangements for Rajah to dress casual and meet me in the west end of the parking lot at the Walmart Super Center on San Mateo behind the Castle Superstore on Central Avenue. From there, Rajah and I would work our way to Interstate-25 and then take a short zip north to Placitas.

"Wow!" Rajah exclaimed. "No one ever said Janet was loaded."

My Hummer slowly rumbled down the crunchy gravel drive to Janet and Steve's big Placitas home in southwestern stucco and style. Steve answered the door and said that Janet was doing the finishing touches on dinner, and he led us into what looked like a commercial kitchen with stainless-steel appliances and such.

With big poofy oven mitts, Janet was holding an obviously heavy and large pan of lasagna. She set the Italian delicacy on the counter and turned to greet us. Janet looked so damned surprised as she slowly and matter-of-factly said, "Well hello Bret...Hello Rajah."

Rajah giggled and Steve obviously had no idea about the drama from work and the months and years leading up to this dinner at Janet's home.

Janet would always put out such a spread with appetizers like antipasto along with lasagna, Italian green beans...I think we had cheesecake for desert or maybe even real Italian cannoli made in-house by Janet. After the long restaurant-caliber dinner was set around the table, we visited with friendly banter.

"Rajah," Janet questioned, serious but not stern, and obviously not approving either. "Where is your husband?"

Rajah looked at me, then down, then at Janet, "He is out of town."

A few days later we learned that Rajah's husband was in prison due to some sort of parole infraction from previous criminal activity. None of us ever knew he had been in jail before. Soon, Rajah's mother would come to get her and the baby to take them to a new home near Portland, Oregon.

It was difficult to absorb the idea that Rajah would move so far away from Albuquerque, but I knew that she had serious personal issues.

"Are you sure you don't want to stay?" I asked Rajah as we embraced in the parking lot outside one day after work.

"Yes Bret," she said stoically. "I need to go."

Rajah had such a colorful life. She told me once that when she was six or seven years old, her dad took the family to Mexico to live. Rajah, her two older brothers, her mom, and her dad lived in a camper parked on the beach. A tiny camper. A camper for the back of a pickup truck. The dad needed to return to California for something, and they removed the camper from the pickup truck. Rajah said that it seemed like her Dad was gone forever and he would never return. The camper just sat in the sand on the beach in Mexico.

On the horizon, purple dark clouds formed over the ocean, and Rajah said that for a few days they watched these clouds get bigger and closer.

About fifty Mexicans from the nearby town walked to the beach. Men with large lumber boards picked up the camper and carried it, on foot, to the nearby town before the storm arrived. Rajah said it was quite a sight watching the men carry the camper by hand and on foot to town…all the way to town. Rajah, her two brothers, and mom could *not* speak Spanish, and yet these Mexicans were so kind in helping them. Small kids and women were running around as the men carried the camper by hand and on foot all the way to town. Rajah said she was little, like six or seven, so the journey seemed like ten miles. Once in town, the Mexicans were very nice, taking turns to deliver meals and food like fresh fruit and vegetables.

Lola and I met Rajah at the Walmart parking lot on San Mateo her final night in Albuquerque. We drove in the Hummer to the Caravan Club on East Central Ave and just laughed and told stories. Rajah was scheduled to work the next day, and we were all planning to go to lunch.

When Rajah's beta fish and small tank was on my credenza near my desk, I knew that the night before was it, and that we would not see Rajah again. It was such a tough day of work to sit there all day, and especially tough when everyone started to go home at the close of their day at 4:30 PM while I had to sit alone until 5:00 P.M. The drive home west on Montano hurt, and I did not even play the radio. Just silence.

One month after Rajah moved away, she sent to my home, a handwritten letter telling me how well she was doing as a receptionist in a doctor's office. She drew little cartoons in the margins of the letter. I scribbled a letter back, and this went on for eight months after Rajah moved away. I helped Rajah divorce her husband with an online divorce kit. I submitted the documents to the Bernalillo County clerk, and Rajah was free from her marriage. She said she would pay me back every penny of the cost to process the divorce, but we lost touch over the years. Even with Myspace and Facebook, I never had any more contact with Rajah.

I would like to think the times Rajah spent with me were just as memorable to her as her living on the beach in Mexico story.

Review and Supplement

I had some correspondence via email with my publisher today asking how soon I would have this book finished. I mentioned that I should have something by Thursday or Friday.

Before I pop out the final two chapters, I would like to take this opportunity to provide a bit of a review for the reader...

Be subtle with women and never commanding. Women are smart, and as soon as we accept that fact, we will perform better in every aspect of our lives.

Be cool and calm...Make friends. Never make the final objective a search and destroy mission for the area between her legs. We are not cavemen only her out to continue mankind. It is okay to be a nice guy.

Never call, text, email or hound her with some sort of communication in a perpetual manner. Obviously, as we are now well into the twenty-first century, we have methods of communication at our fingertips, and it can only grow from here. Do not contact her every time a thought pops into your head, she does not need to see that sandwich you had for lunch at Twin Peaks today. Think you fool...Think.

Social media can be great, and social media can be your downfall. Use with caution. *Think* before you post, and know that less is more. With mystery comes curiosity, and if you put too much out there, no one will be interested in getting to learn about you and to get to know you.

Look nice and smell nice—use a small splash of cologne—wear nice clothes, drive a nice car, have a nice job. One should not live a fantasy life from examples from Hollywood movies…However, watch for examples of how people act, dress, and such. A great movie production has art directors, and there is a reason why people wear certain shirts with certain shoes and drive a certain car and so on.

Read books and read often: *How to Win Friends and Influence People* by Dale Carnegie and *The Art of War* by Sun Tzu. There are some contemporary books to consider as well, like *The Subtle Art of Not Giving a F**** by Mark Mansen and *You are a Bad ASS* by Jen Sincero. She actually graduated with ME in the class of 1987 at The Colorado College. I probably served her dinner in the Bemis/Taylor Dining Hall during my brief job with SAGA-Marriott. Instead of the khaki pants with the uniform polo shirt and blue logo ball cap, I was the guy in the US Army issue desert camo pants and a crushed New York Yankee cap. Do You remember me, Jen? I also worked in the dining hall with then-Wyoming Senator Dick Cheney's daughter Liz. We worked a lot together, and she was a cool friend and just another college kid. Her mother Lynne was our commencement speaker for graduation. Crazy how we all moved out in the world. (I still have those US Army issue desert camo pants.)

You must read *The Secret* so that you can learn all about The Law of Attraction. There is *no* such thing as a coincidence, and you will see how people and events become connected and related in your exciting life. This stuff really works…Hence, I am about to complete my second published book for *you*.

If you just cannot make the time to read, get books on audio or at least look for condensed YouTube videos. YouTube has become one of my best friends. I have YouTube videos playing constantly as I drive in the car. I seldom have the radio on anymore.

YouTube channels I watch all started with the goofy Amber Scholl. I am hooked. I also watch AlphaM, Gentlemen's Gazette, Real Men Real Style, How to Beast with David de los Morenas, Dave Perrotta, Arica Angelo, Apollonia Ponti, Buff Bunny, School of Affluence with Anna Bey…and many others.

Get your ass out of bed before 5:00 A.M. Get moving and start your day…*Everyday*. Make the bed each and every day. Do not dispute this and do not ask why. *Just* do it. *Never* say I cannot do that. *Yes* you can, but first you must try.

Failing is a big part of success. Every successful person has failed over and over.

Understand that there will be haters. I have had envious people long before I published my first book, and now I have numerous others, always critical, with the goal to put me in my place.

Go to school or college if that works for *you*…and finish what you start with a degree. None of this shit about, "I can't afford it…I don't have time…"

Watch the Arnold Schwarzenegger video on YouTube about his life. He just sits there and tells the viewer what he did and how he did it. No one gets anywhere bitching, complaining, and attempting to validate why they cannot do something.

Get fired up and grab the world by the balls and create adventure and the best life *you* can.

Ask open-ended questions. Instead of "How was your Valentine's Day?" ask "What was the best part of your Valentine's?"

Never ever treat a woman like a trophy…This goes with no additional required explanation.

Do not give to get. Give and provide favors with no reason to expect anything in return.

Trust…

As Maya Angelou said, "People may forget what you said, but people will always remember how you made them feel."

I understand not everyone will graduate from college, have a sweet home with no roommates, have cool dishes and barware like in the movies, and drive a big yellow H2 Hummer just exactly like the Hummer on the hit HBO Series *Entourage*. Not everyone can have a dream job that pays well with a car allowance, cool office, great pay, and an expense account for power lunches and fun stuff. I understand that not just anyone can run out and purchase a Range Rover Sport HSE during the lunch hour and then allow a twenty-year-old woman from Twin Peaks to start driving the vehicle and subsequently moving into your home with all her clothes and stuff...*and* she has a lot of fucking clothes and stuff. I lost track how many trips she made in that Range Rover just to move her stuff into my home, but it was a lot.

Crazy stuff starts with crazy ideas and affirmations to the universe before you can actually go out and make it happen.

While attending The Colorado College, we were required to study courses out of the WASP (White Anglo-Saxon Protestant) typical college-university curriculum and hence, I learned so much about Eastern Religion and Philosophy. Hence, I have a Zen garden with a Buddha statue in my yard. Never be afraid to learn something new.

I may be going out on a limb here, but if you watch TV, be sure to watch *Shark Tank* as well as *Keeping Up with The Kardashians*. If you understand it...great. If you do not get it...never be a critical piss-poor hater, and maybe you should just move on. Kourtney and her sisters drive around in fancy Range Rovers with big mansion homes, nice clothes, and they go out for power lunches, they travel, and make money...They are happy. They obviously *know* what they are doing. Before you say something stupid like our former President Obama... THINK...and it may be best to say nothing at all and figure out how you can live just like Kourtney and her sisters.

Use examples, and do your best. If You think Bret is a fool, think about the royalties I make from these books, which are about mere stories covering me while I was already being paid a fat salary to do my job with that big stucco company. Do not hate, and do not feel bad.

Know that *you can* do great things and have a super life while you *keep a woman happy.*

Now…let's wrap this up and proceed with the final two chapters.

Chapter Seven
Attend an All-Woman Party

I had been rumbling around in the big nasty yellow H2 Hummer for just over two years when I received a call one July afternoon from Felicia that things were slow at Hooters, and she was working the patio if I had time for lunch. It was a Friday, and I actually did not have lunch that day as 1:00 P.M. was approaching. Most people goof off on Friday and are not available too much. I have always been out and about especially, on Fridays while others are MIA, and I never do the blue jeans casual Friday. On Friday I break out the best of my Ralph Lauren dress Oxford shirts and dress slacks. I think I had on a crisp super-bright white Ralph Lauren Oxford shirt.

I could not convince anyone to join me for lunch, and as I just mentioned…others were not to be found.

Once I located a seat on the patio and started to munch on my chicken quesadillas with extra guacamole, I did remember my insurance agent Steven. He was in his late twenties and a single Dad. After a quick text message, he was with me on the patio at Hooters on San Mateo in Albuquerque, New Mexico enjoying lunch. He was uptight like a bug was up his ass from being nervous.

"Felicia," I said, waving her over to my table. "I need to bail by three so I can get to my office and spend some desk time until 5:00 P.M."

"Okay buddy, you want your check now?" Felicia asked.

Since we had no booze, just iced tea with free refills and we did not plan to order more food, Felicia closed out my bill.

"Hey buddy," Felicia started. "You doing anything fun tonight?"

"Naw, nothing much." I responded with confidence, knowing that she had more to ask.

"You want to come to a cookout in the South Valley?" Felicia asked with a wink of her left eye.

"Sure…South Valley…Your parent's house?" I inquired, knowing this was leading up to something FUN!

"Nope," Felicia slapped my arm. "It's at my new girlfriend's place."

"Wow!" I sat up straight in my seat on the patio at Hooters that hot July afternoon. "I would love to…"

With that, Felicia tore off a sheet of paper towel which is located on each table at every Hooters location. She scribbled with her pen a rudimentary map.

"Okay buddy…This is your house, " Felicia pointed to her map. "Drive all the way down Unser, move over to Coors until Barcelona, then turn towards the mountains past the Mushroom Store and up the First Street West. It's got a huge football field of grass and a long gravel drive…"

Felicia went to attend a few other tables, and Steven my insurance agent looked puzzled and took the paper towel map from my hands.

"How does she know where *you* live?" Steven asked.

"Felicia?" I looked at Steven. "She has been serving beer at our golf tourney with the Home Builders Association for a couple years now."

"But why does she know where *you* live?" Steven asked.

"She has been my house sitter before when I traveled out of town," I replied, sipping my iced tea.

Felicia returned to our table. "So buddy, you coming tonight?"

"Do I need to bring anything? Ketchup, mustard, other con-
diments…anything?" I asked.

"Nope, we will just steal that stuff from here like always when we
have parties and stuff," Felicia laughed.

"So it's mainly Hooters girls coming tonight?" I said with a smile
to Felicia but looking at Steven my insurance agent.

"Yep, most of us girls from Hooters…Roxy for sure…a few other
girls like Mariana, that Russian girl who does not work here anymore
because they fired her." Felicia said, dancing around our table picking
up the dirty plates from our lunch. "You're not going to eat your
pickle?" Felicia asked Steven as he just shook his head with the side-
to-side international no symbol.

"Let me get this straight," Steven looked at me. "You are going
to a party tonight with all Hooters women…tonight?"

"That's how it looks," I said with a grin. "And I will probably be
one of the only men at the party."

Felicia returned to our table with a pitcher of iced tea and filled
our glasses.

"Will there be any other guys at the party tonight?" I asked
Felicia.

"Nope…just *you* buddy…the only guy." Felicia laughed, and she
went to wait on another table.

"Just you…the only guy…" Steven mumbled to himself.

"Would *you* want to go?" I asked as I handed the paper towel map
to Steven. "Here are the directions. Felicia won't mind."

"Naw…I don't have anyone to watch my kids," Steven replied,
disappointed.

"I know you want to go to this all-Hooters-women party." I used
my famous George Clooney cool demeanor. "You should see some of
these ladies in their street clothes. Mmm…And they will be drinking
and *no* other guys around. You should go!"

"Felicia, are you sure that I will be the only man?" I asked and continued. "There will be *no* boyfriends?"

"No boyfriends and *no* boys," Felicia smiled and punched my arm. "Can you handle that?"

YSC ! You're So Cool!

I did break down and go to Walmart for a big-ass bottle of Jose Cuervo along with pre-made bottles of both strawberry and lime margarita mix. I dressed in one of my Lacoste polo shirts—I love that little crocodile—khaki shorts and hiking boots. I rumbled down the long, long, crunchy, crushed gravel driveway at the South Valley home of Felicia's girlfriend. There were big, fat hundred-year-old Cottonwood trees that I swear the Keebler Elves live inside of on each boundary of the shady driveway. Despite being July, it was a cool Friday evening, and I was ready to party.

There were not too many women at the party when I arrived at around 8:00 P.M. while the sun had not yet set on the horizon. I placed the big-ass bottle of Jose Cuervo with pre-mixed bottles of Margarita mix on an open space of the counter top in the kitchen next to a Hooters plastic to-go bag filled with *new* mustard, ketchup, hot sauce, and other items.

The home was sleek, like a display from IKEA. Hardwood floor with a white sofa sectional and shaggy white rug. On the far wall was a giant flat-screen TV with other electronic and stereo space-age stuff on a huge blonde wood shelf unit from floor to ceiling.

Felicia introduced me to her girlfriend, and for the life of me I cannot recall her name. It was her home, and she had some sort of professional job with great pay. She had a *full* stocked bar with the ability to make just about any drink one could order from the bar of a big hotel found in any major city.

There was a real cutie pie server from Hooters who was also at the party. DAMN OMG she was so super HOT, just like Arianna Grande even before Ms. Grande was a star on Nickelodeon and certainly long before the "God is a Woman" hit song. Her girlfriend was one of those girls with the baggy loose blue jeans, flannel shirt, Doc Marten boots, and a buzz cut so short she had whiskers in a five o'clock shadow on the side of her head. She was nice and shook my hand with her chewed up stubby fingers as she said an enthusiastic "Hello!"

"How You doin' tonight? What was the *best* part of your week?" I asked, looking at both ladies and making eye contact back and forth while thinking, *Why does she have a girlfriend like that when there are guys who look like that and they cannot ever get a girlfriend?* (Okay, by now you may have wondered and pondered. Remember, I met Felicia through Rachel, and Rachel did not have a boyfriend. Rachel had a girlfriend, and she lived with her girlfriend. Go back a few chapters and review. Re-read if you forgot.) Yes, Felicia was a lesbian, and she had never been with a man. Felicia's panty dropper Ford Mustang was parked near my big nasty yellow H2 Hummer on the crunchy, crushed gravel driveway. "Panty dropper" was always the description applied to that Hot Rod Mustang from Ford by Felicia herself...NOT by me.

One could not make up shit like this...Yes, I was attending an all-women party in the South Valley of Albuquerque, New Mexico at a private IKEA-inspired home on a cool Friday evening in July.

"This is that cool guy who hangs out with Felicia at Hooters I was telling you about," shouted the Arianna Grande cutie pie. "It's Bret, right? You are Bret?"

"Are you gay?" asked another of the lesbians dressed in khaki pants and a red flannel shirt with black Chuck Taylor Converse basketball shoes. She too had short nails on her fingers. I always notice hands, and I love a woman with manicured nails.

"No," I answered, George Clooney cool. "I am hetro." I switched to an Arnold Schwarzenegger accent like in the old movie *Total Recall* as he was going under for his dream sequence implant.

"Aw...heterosexual!" the Chuck Taylor lesbian said in a smart-ass tone, correcting me with the proper vernacular. "Are we sure we are not straight? There will be some *straight* women here at the party?"

"I noticed that lesbians have very short fingernails." I continued in friendly conversation with the Chuck Taylor lesbian and with the Arianna Grande girl as well as her five o'clock shadow girlfriend looking on, seemingly interested in my topic. "Do you lesbians all have short fingernails out of convenience or courtesy?"

The Chuck Taylor lesbian looked at me directly in the eye and said, "Oh Felicia, I love your friend."

"Oh that's cool." Felicia said, approaching us from across the room. "Did Bret tell you he is on the board of directors at the zoo, and he is the president of some women thing...and what is it you do with the Home Builders' Association...board of directors there too?"

We all sort of meandered outside on a cool shady patio. Felicia's girlfriend would make drinks in cycles...a round of vodka martinis, then gin and tonic...old-fashioned...and so on. When I suggested that it was not such a good idea to mix all these different drinks, no one paid any attention to me.

The big-ass bottle of Jose Cuervo and pre-mixed bottles of both strawberry and lime margarita mix went untouched all night. Never go to a party emptyhanded...flowers, a bottle of wine... bread...You must take something, and do not get insulted if your gift goes untouched.

The lesbians were having difficulty lighting the gas grill outside when the Chuck Taylor Lesbian kept trying to use a cigarette Bic lighter, reaching deep into the grill.

"That is not a good idea," I said to her.

"Well get your swinging limp dick over here and light this bitch so we can eat!" exclaimed the Chuck Taylor lesbian.

"I use a charcoal grill," I answered with distinction. "I am not familiar with a gas grill."

"Felicia, "your man" is useless!" yelled the Chuck Taylor lesbian. Everyone laughed.

"Felicia" I started. "Where the *hell* is Roxy? Isn't she coming? Any other Hooters women? Any single women? I had no idea that little tiny girl who looks like a Disney princess was a lesbian."

"Oh no, Roxy can't make it, but there will be other girls coming," Felicia said. "Mariana the Russian girl said she would show. Hooters fired her, and now she is doing stand-up comedy and training as a server at Olive Garden."

"Fired?" I blurted out. "Fired? How did Mariana get fired at Hooters?"

Felicia laughed and answered, "They said she was too fat."

"What? Too Fat...Hooters can fire you if you get too fat?" I asked.

"Yep buddy. Too fat was the reason they fired Mariana," Felicia laughed.

"Aw fuck, I wish You had not told me that," I laughed back. "Now it will be difficult to face her."

"Well...you asked me why Mariana got fired." Felicia laughed more.

"Too Fat," I said.

"Too Fat," Felicia affirmed as she shook her head.

The Lesbians eventually gave up on the gas grill, and Felicia's girlfriend made hot dogs and burgers in a big skillet on the stove inside the kitchen of the IKEA-inspired home. Soon there was the smell of burger grease like the concession stand at a bowling alley, and the kitchen was full of cooking smoke with the crashing sizzle sound of animal flesh searing on a scorching hot skillet.

"Who wants a hot dog?" yelled Felicia. "They don't take long to cook and will be ready soon."

"This is the only time I want a fucking weiner!" yelled the Chuck Taylor lesbian as she looked me dead in the eye, snapping her jaw shut like a great white shark.

Not to get off track here, but all of the women at the party had movie star, pearly white, perfect teeth. I notice teeth for some strange reason. Not anything to do with the story...just an observation. I should have become an orthodontist. Oh well, my BA in Fine Arts degree from The Colorado College has served me well over the years.

The Chuck Taylor lesbian had a weiner with no bun in her hands, swinging and flapping the big pink phallic around and giving me dirty looks...ripping off shark bites of the pink meat and chewing up the ground-up pink weiner with her mouth open...Oh Hell. I guess that remark about the short finger nails pissed her off. I hope she does not get bored and try to castrate me with some of those fancy cutlery items I noticed hanging on a magnetic strip over the stove. Felicia would never allow any harm to come to me. They refer to me as "her man" anyway.

We started to play video games in the wee hours of midnight. I was dominating Wii bowling. The fried burger stench, like a bowling alley concession stand, must have put me in the mood. Mariana had arrived at some point in time, and I wanted to ask her so bad about why she got fired at Hooters. She had a Marilyn Monroe figure... nothing I would describe as fat, and certainly not grounds for termination at Hooters of all places, for fawk sake. It may have been the bra she was wearing, but her big boobs were very firm and round.

"They fucking fired me because I'm too fat," Mariana was overheard telling one of the lesbians. "Can you fucking believe that?" Mariana was still wearing the white blouse of an Olive Garden server, where she was now training, and had obviously driven direct to the all-women party in the South Valley of Albuquerque on a cool Friday night in July.

"What? Too Fat? Really? "I questioned, as if this were the very first time I had heard the topic. "Last time I noticed you working at Hooters, you looked amazing in your uniform."

"Thanks!" Mariana looked at me and only now noticed that a man was present. "And fawk Hooters...Are You that guy who comes in on Saturday and sits out on the patio with all of those Victoria's Secret catalogs?"

"Yeah...He is Felicia's friend," someone yelled.

"I know he is Felicia's friend," Mariana yelled back. "I need to get a new bra or two...My boobs have been getting bigger. Do you have any of those Victoria's Secret catalogs with you?"

"No...not tonight." I said, not skipping a beat and dominating with Wii bowling.

At one point I played with Mariana on my team. We kept chest bumping...No lie...Why would I lie? Wii bowling was so fun at that party. Yeah, if you must know, her boobs were spectacular. Mariana and I kept beating the shit out of all those who played us, and we continued to chest bump after each bowling frame. I was concentrating on Wii bowling and constantly watching so that the Chuck Taylor lesbian did not sneak up from behind me and knock me unconscious with that big greasy skillet her wiener was fried in earlier that evening.

"Bret met President Bush!" yelled Felicia to no one in particular.

"Bullshit!" someone yelled.

"Why don't You just marry him if you love him so much?" yelled another.

"President Bush?" someone asked.

"No you dumb fuck...Bret," yelled someone else.

"Felicia doesn't like boys," yelled another. "You don't like bush either do you?'

"The between-the-legs hoo hah Bush or the president of the United States Bush?" someone smarted off.

"What do you fucking think...both!" another women yelled. "No Bush...ever. Hate it...nasty."

"Hey...she *is* correct," I interrupted. "I did meet President Bush at a function at the state fairgrounds during a Home Builders' Association event. And, it's true. Felicia does not like boys."

"You fucking liar," yelled the Chuck Taylor lesbian. "And Felicia doesn't love you. She won't marry you...and you shouldn't even be here."

"Felicia isn't my type," I said in my famous George Clooney cool. "I like women with long, slender, manicured nails, and I have always been turned on by a mohawk-trimmed bush, but seems like ladies now prefer to shave it all off. Makes sense. Shave the pits and shave the legs...shave the entire bush too."

"Fawk you!" said the Chuck Taylor lesbian. "You will never know if Felicia has a bush or not."

"President Bush shook my hand," I smarted off.

"The same hand you beat off your fat weiner with," The Chuck Taylor lesbian yelled back.

"Yeah so...the Secret Service was there." I had nothing and did not know how to reply, especially after she chewed up that wiener with her mouth open only a few short hours prior. Damn, we needed to get off the subject of weiners as well as the hate displayed for me. No matter what I said, this Chuck Taylor lesbian flat did not want me at the party.

I slept on the sofa sectional alone, with sheets and pillow provided by Felicia. Obviously Felicia and her girlfriend slept in the master bedroom. No idea where Mariana slept, but it was her creeping on the hardwood floors sneaking out quietly to work her 11 A.M. training shift at Olive Garden that woke me from my slumber. Man oh man, was I ever sick to my stomach...Ick!

Driving in reverse my big nasty yellow H2 Hummer, just like the Hummer on the hit HBO series *Entourage*, down the long, crunchy, crushed gravel driveway with hundred-year-old fat large Cottonwood trees was no easy accomplishment with a sour stomach and pounding head from an all-night, all-women party in the South Valley of Albuquerque, New Mexico on a cool Friday night/early Saturday morning in July. Pardon my French, but all I wanted to do was just puke... à la vomit.

Felicia was and is one of my most cool and colorful friends to this day. She has assisted in serving beer at my hospitality/major sponsor tent for the Home Builders' Association every summer for over a decade.

Chapter Eight
Support and Respect Her Adventure

Minami had most of her super-full class schedule for her final semester prior to graduation at the University of New Mexico as online
courses. Other than the typical evening 4 P.M. to close shift on Friday
and Saturday at Twin Peaks, as well as her daily gym training sessions
for her bikini fitness competition and the occasional visit to her parents' home, Minami was at my house on a perpetual basis. Minami
was very comfortable in my home, and she was certainly moved in as
permanent as could be described.

"You have the yummiest food here, Bret," Said Minami as her
105-pound body would eat four bananas, scrambled egg whites, spinach, brussels sprouts, shrimp, and so on. Minami had, by this point,
meal-prep sponsors, a few clothing sponsors, and even a teeth-whitening sponsor. Minami brushed her teeth at least four times per day,
and her smile was perhaps my favorite feature on her.

She was in the cutting stages of her bikini fitness competition,
and I ate the same food as she did in my best effort to be supportive...except those fucking brussels sprouts. Gawd, I tried. I did the
scrambled egg whites with lots of Valentina Mexican hot sauce and
turkey sausages.

I have a weakness for Reese's Peanut Butter Cups, and Minami would ask that I not buy them and place them in the giant stainless-steel fridge, like the appliances one has on the MTV show *Cribs* or *Keeping Up with The Kardashians.*

It was so much fun eating with chop sticks as Minami would tell me about the best part of her courses in school or the best part of her gym training.

"Hey Bret," Minami started as she ate a few brussels sprouts and cold shrimp with her chop sticks, dipping them in a puddle of siracha sauce on her plate. "Know how you told me that there was no tax refund on your return this year and you were required to pay?"

"Yes Minami...how could I forget?" I asked.

"Well, my economics professor was praising the new Trump tax laws, and they are so wonderful."Minami said, smart, educated, and matter of fact. "Do you want to know what my professor said?"

"Sure Minami," I sighed. "Please tell me what your UNM economics professor said about Bret's taxes."

"He said," Minami, like a little astute woman, continued. "The only people not getting decent tax refunds this year under the new Trump tax laws are millionaires. Your friend must be a millionaire."

"Whatever, you caught me!" I laughed and raised my hands up.

Minami would have marathon study sessions but ask that I get her up early. I would always wake between 4:30 A.M. and 5:00 A.M. each and every day with *no* alarm clock. I started to wake Minami at about 6:30 A.M., as I would depart for work, and off to the gym she went in either cool Nike gear I had purchased or gym wear provided by a sponsor. Soon, she would wake at the same time as me, at 5:00 A.M. I would always work on a few computer email job-related duties and check my sales numbers bright and early, and then between 6:00 and 6:30 A.M. , shave, get dressed, make the bed, and off to work. During these super-early morning hours, Minami would play Anthony Robbins blogs from YouTube or other motivational speakers. Minami would also play wild songs like *Walking on Sunshine* by Katrina and The Waves because it was in the movie *Daddy Daycare*. Minami would also play *Rather Be* by Clean Bandit, along with assorted Ariana Grande music, since Ms. Grande was crushing the music charts at the time. *God is a Woman*. Minami was so very cute first thing in the morning with her sleepy Japanese eyes and messy thick hair. Around the house, she was either in her gym wear or plain t-shirts and tiny athletic shorts. Early in the A.M. I would kiss her forehead.

"Did You just kiss my head?" Minami would laugh, looking at me with her sleepy Japanese eyes. "The forehead is the mind's eye."

YSC! You're So Cool!

"Hey Bret!" Minami yelled across the mid-century, modern living room with dry-stack-ledge stone all the way up the vaulted ceiling. "You should see some of my posing routines for the fitness competition."

"I would love to see them," I responded, and then asked. "Do You need a bikini sponsor?" We were spending Sunday evening watching a *Shark Tank* marathon on MSNBC. Minami contends that *Shark Tank* is her favorite show. I had purchased a Lori Greiner power dress in solid black as a Xmas gift for Minami and told her she could wear said dress when she would certainly appear on *Shark Tank* soon in the future.

On her smart phone, Minami began to seek numerous bikini websites for fitness competitions. After looking at what seemed to be hundreds of pictures of fitness women in competition bikinis, we decided on a maroon color, and I paid the ridiculous five hundred dollar price. Oh well...

It was the month of March, and absolutely everything was on target...University graduation and the fitness competition were on the calendar.

She parked "her" Range Rover Sport back-end into the garage next to the big nasty yellow H2 Hummer, and the all-black Chevy Tahoe was parked in the driveway. When I heard the automatic garage door open at around 3:00 A.M. after her Twin Peaks closing shifts, I would always get excited. Minami would wind down with a shower, remove her make up, and usually eat something light. I would get up out of bed and visit with her at times.

Minami would leave me goofy notes all around the house on tiny yellow legal pads. Goofy stuff like "Hey Bret–Guess What?" on a note found on the wall by the bedroom door. Then on another note in the kitchen, "YSC! You're SO COOL!" Or the ever-popular, "There are chicken tenders in the fridge." Minami would also sign her notes with YFA. (Your Favorite Asian) or YFLA (Your Favorite Little Asian). Minami would text those goofy "YSC! You're SO COOL" messages as well from time to time on her smart phone.

We had both read the book by Jen Sincero, *You are a Bad Ass*, and we kept telling each other that all the freaking time.

"Hey Bret...you know what?" Minami would ask, looking up from her Apple laptop. "You Are a Bad Ass!"

Minami had given me an Echo Dot for Xmas, and we would have that device repeat goofy stuff as well.

"Echo," I would say. "Simon says, Minami is a Bad Ass!" And thus the Echo Dot device would repeat what I said in her pleasant woman's voice.

"Minami is a bad ass!"

"No, you're a Bad Ass!" Minami would laugh, smile, and argue.

"Well, you're so cool!" I would respond and laugh.

Minami was on top of the world, and I enjoyed watching.

For the first time in her life, she went on a trip to Las Vegas, Nevada as a member of the entourage for MMA fighter Diego Sanchez. I drove her to the Albuquerque airport for departure and collected her upon the return flight. "What was the *best* part of your Vegas trip?" I asked Minami.

With sleepy eyes, standing near the baggage claim, Minami said, "I had such a blast, Bret. Diego won his fight, and all of us girls did a lot of photo shoots over the weekend. We took a billion pictures."

The following Friday night, Minami sent a text message while she was working a closing shift at Twin Peaks. "You want some food?"

I sent a simple reply text, "Sure."

"You got it dude," Minami sent back in her return text.

Damn she was so much fun, and we had become so comfortable together since we had first met the year before on the Saturday right after Valentine's Day. My book that Minami had encouraged me to write, called *How to Make a Woman Happy* had been published, and we were patiently waiting for the first copy to arrive.

All I heard out of Minami was, "I want to read it, Bret." And this went on for well over six months during the book publication process: edits, page layout, and cover design.

"You get the first copy," I would explain to Minami. "I want *you* to read the actual book itself in your hands."

YSC! You're So Cool!

I was watching on TV the weekly video countdown on BET Jams when the T-Pain video, at number six, was on. "Hey Minami...get out here quick...You are on TV in that T-Pain music video!" I yelled, sitting on the green L-shaped sofa sectional in my mid-century, modern living room with dry-stack-ledge stone all the way up to the vaulted ceiling.

"Okay," Minami responded in a sweet soft polite voice. "Take a picture for me." She was once again in the front spare bedroom that we used as an office, printing a homework assignment.

"You are such a bad ass!" I laughed. "Your humble hard-as-a-rock tight little Asian ass is so humble. Have you even seen this T-Pain music video on TV yet?"

"No…you're a bad ass!" Minami yelled back.

"That makes *no* sense," I laughed. "Why am I a bad ass?"

"You just are. It was your Wells Fargo Visa Platinum card that paid for my boobs from Scottsdale," Minami laughed.

Yes…last summer, in July, for Minami's twenty-first birthday, I had placed her on my Wells Fargo Platinum Visa with her name stamped on her own card. "Go ahead and get some boobs in Scotts-dale. Just keep it all under ten grand."

We actually first met the Saturday right after Valentine's while she was working an afternoon shift at Twin Peaks. I gave her my business card…We started texting. I went back to Twin Peaks a couple more times but did not sit in her section. I was around, but not too much.

In May, one week before I purchased the sweet Range Rover Sport, Minami and I crashed the Twin Peaks bikini carwash. We met at PF Chang's across from Twin Peaks, and much to everyone's sur-prise, Minami drove up to have the big nasty yellow H2 Hummer washed. I gave Minami a Range Rover logo key chain and told her to use the Law of Attraction and make affirmations to the universe.

The very day the sweet Range Rover Sport was purchased, I re-quested a ride via text message from Minami. One look at the Range Rover in my driveway, and she asked, "Can I drive that to class later?" I put Minami on my insurance for all of my vehicles. Minami began to drive the Range Rover, and it was referred to as "her" Range Rover.

My good, wise millionaire friend Peggy and I were at a business lunch one day on the patio at Bravo! Italian in the Up Town Center, and when I explained my current events, Peggy exclaimed, "Range Rover? Do *you* make Range Rover kind of money?"

I asked Minami to stay at my home while I was on a business trip in Dallas for a few days, and she fell in love with the place. She sent text messages that she wanted to just move in. She sent selfies to me on her smart phone laying on the verdant lawn adjacent to the Koi pond in my Zen garden. Since her Pops was from Japan, Minami loved the teachings of Buddha, and my Buddha statute in the Zen garden captured her attention.

Now that she had a key to my home, she dropped by often. When the lease expired on her apartment, she briefly moved back in with her parents…and then in with me at my home as my house guest.

When the Range Rover…I mean when "her" Range Rover, was in the shop getting new brakes, I encouraged her to drive the big nasty yellow H2 Hummer for her shift at Twin Peaks. The vehicle was stolen, parked across from Twin Peaks at the PF Chang's parking lot (ironic), recovered the same night, and impounded by the Albuquerque Police. I remained George Clooney cool during the entire time.

I made such serious trust points with Minami when the Hummer was stolen.

I purchased about three hundred boutique-style wooden hangers for all of Minami's clothes. She had quite literally transformed my Asian-themed guest room into a walk-in closet.

Minami encouraged me to write the book *How to Make a Woman Happy* as we were in the kitchen having spinach and crab meat with chop sticks one evening.

YSC! You're So Cool!

As I have mentioned before: Why should the Kardashians have all the fun? Okay…Okay…Back to the month of March of this year.

Actually, let's go to Monday, the first of April, known as April Fools' Day.

I arrived home from work at around 5:45 P.M. and parked the all-black Chevy Tahoe in the driveway, and as the automatic garage door rose up, I was happy to see "her" Range Rover parked in the garage next to the big nasty yellow H2 Hummer. I always enter via the garage. I ran across the street to the group mailbox. Kind of a pain in the ass, but the US mail does not deliver to each individual home in my neighborhood. Hence, I ran across the street and around the corner to get the mail.

Bang! There it was: *How to Keep a Woman Happy*. The first copy from the publisher. I sneaked the book into the house while Minami was taking a shower. I swear I cannot stress enough how Minami is in a perpetual state of bliss and in a good mood all the time…and I mean always.

I scribbled something on the inside front cover. "Minami–Since you know the author, the story will NOT surprise You. YSC! XoXo Bret"

I had dedicated the book itself to Minami.

When she came out of the shower wrapped in a crisp, white giant towel she said, "Hey Bret, guess what? My shoes for the fitness competition arrived FedEx today."

"Minami, get dressed," I said, stern. "You and I need to talk."

"Okay." Minami looked puzzled. "Am I in trouble?"

"Just get some clothes on and come into the office please." I was rather enjoying my stern and stoic performance.

Minami had on a t-shirt and her tiny athletic shorts as she sat in the chair next to the desk where I was seated. "Am I in trouble?'

I burst out laughing. "*You* get the first copy, as promised." And I handed her the book.

She sprang up to her cute bare feet. "Wow, this is real." Minami then read the dedication to her and thumbed through the book. "I can't wait to read this Bret, and *you* are the first author I have ever met."

"And *you*, Minami, are the first protagonist of a book that I have ever met," I sarcastically stated.

It was so cool. The publisher had sent out all kinds of press releases as well as promo copies of the book. I had a case of fifty promo copies sent to my home later that week from the publisher. Amazon, Barnes and Noble, as well as quite a few other online book sellers had MY book for sale.

It was unreal. Minami and I had lived such a cool life over the past year.

YSC! You're So Cool!

Since my Reece's Peanut Butter Cups were to Minami like Kryptonite is to Superman, and since she was in her final stages for the Fitness Competition, I had purchased some SnackWell's cookies instead. Minami was hardly eating anything all day each day, and I did my best to be supportive and hardly eat anything as well.

Damn, her little body was so tight. "I really think you have a shot at this competition."

"I hope so," Minami would say with a smile. "My trainer thinks I could actually take first place."

This was the absolute first time Minami had ever entered such a competition.

As she would stand near the kitchen sink and make her powdered protein shakes, what I referred to as astronaut food, her defined frame was impressive.

I would trace her six pack upon her tight tummy with my index finger as she would chug her shake. I would rub her thigh and down to her calf. Her biceps and triceps had such definition, and yet she still maintained a woman's figure. I kissed her forehead.

"Did you just kiss my head?" Minami laughed. "That is my mind's eye."

I had sent a promo copy of my book to my mom in Sterling, Colorado. My Mom had NO idea the big nasty yellow H2 Hummer had been stolen. I owned a sweet Range Rover Sport. My mom did not even know about Minami, let alone that Minami was my house guest living in my home for nearly a year now.

I had done UPS tracking, and when I knew the package had been delivered but I had no response from my mom, I was compelled to telephone. Now remember, I call my parents every Saturday morning at 6:00 A.M. sharp, and we visit for about an hour. My mom would often get irate and say, "Why are you speaking so softly? I can't hear you Bret!" I could not tell my mom that Minami lived with me and that she got home at 3:00 A.M. after a closing Twin Peaks shift and even though she was super smart and ready to graduate from the University of New Mexico in just a few short weeks with *three* bachelor's degrees…My mom would certainly *not* understand.

It was a Wednesday evening, and I phoned about ten minutes after 6:00 P.M. My mom answered the phone in a goofy and sarcastic tone. "Yeees?"

"Did you…ahm…ah…get a UPS package today?" I nervously asked.

"Sure did," Mom blurted out. "It's funny as *hell*, and I'm on chapter seven already. But buddy…you and I need to talk this Saturday."

On Saturday, my mom said, "That book makes you look like a dumb ass. How much of that is true?"

"Well, I may look like a dumb ass, but as the actual writer," I continued. "I will be the one paid royalties."

"Bret, did *you* really buy that little girl a Range Rover?" Mom asked disapprovingly.

"*You* are not paying attention to the book, " I replied. "I bought a Range Rover, and Minami drives it."

"Minami," Mom added. "At first I thought she was another one of your black girlfriends...What was that one girl's name? Rajah?"

"Minami is part Japanese and part Italian," I said simply.

"YOU did NOT actually buy her BOOBS, did YOU?" Mom asked.

"Mom, it's just a book...and it's already popular and doing well." With that I directed her to Amazon, Barnes and Noble, as well as other fine book sellers.

YSC! You're So Cool!

When I heard the automatic garage door go up and "her" Range Rover back in, I squinted at my alarm clock and noticed it was just after 3:00 A.M. Despite a lot of extra noise in the kitchen and during her shower, I did not get out of bed. Minami really was crashing around in the kitchen much more than usual.

Each Sunday morning I type up a brief sales and activity recap of the week for my regional director Joe and send it via email. Doing this action on Sunday for really only a few minutes time just helps start Monday on a good footing, and it keeps the numbers sharp in my head.

I was finished with my report to Joe and was quietly watching YouTube videos when Minami was standing in the hall—sleepy Japanese eyes, messy hair, and bare feet, wearing a t-shirt and her tiny athletic shorts. At first I thought she was trying to be funny. . . .

"Bret, I had a meltdown and ate a whole box of cookies, and I'm so stressed." Minami had tears in her sleepy Japanese eyes, and her voice was cracking.

"What's wrong?" I stood up.

Minami grabbed me and wrapped her arms around my ribs, plunging her head into my chest. "My mom is in the hospital, Bret. My sister tried to call me, but I didn't have my phone with me at work."

"Shhh...It's okay. Be strong...Be strong, " I whispered, kissing her forehead.

"I am strong," Minami said, crying. "I don't know if I can keep living here Bret."

"Minami, call your sister and find out if your mom is home or still in the hospital. Get cleaned up, take a shower, and go home." I softly spoke

"I love living here with *you*, Bret...It's so much fun here." Minami still cried.

"It will be okay, Minami, " I held her. "If it were very serious, your sister would have actually gone to Twin Peaks or called Twin Peaks...not just leave you a message on your phone."

"I have finals coming up, and graduation, the competition...I am so stressed," Minami cried.

I just held her tight. "It will be all okay...Get cleaned up and let me know if you need me for anything."

"I just want to live a normal life," Minami sobbed.

"There is no such thing as a normal life, Minami...There is just life." I found myself quoting Val Kilmer as Doc Holiday from the movie *Tombstone*.

Minami was gone all day and returned in the late evening just to grab a few of her things and let me know her mom was at home from the hospital and doing well. Minami told me that she would stay at her parent's home that night. I never asked why her mom was in the hospital...kind of a Buddha thing to care but not need details.

On Monday evening, Minami returned and made herself some food in the kitchen. "I may need to drop out of the competition, Bret."

"Aw Minami…All that hard work and the diet and the training… Only *you* know what is best," I said in my George Clooney cool. "I think after a day or two you will be back on track."

"I am going to stay at my parent's again tonight," Minami informed me almost in the form of a question.

"Minami do what *you* feel is best. No need to check in with me," I told her.

Over the course of the next few days, Minami managed to get most of her things moved out and back to her parent's home. Each day when I came home from work there were cute little yellow notes for me and evidence that Minami had eaten in the kitchen.

When I noticed virtually all of her products, soaps, toothpaste, and such gone from the bathroom, I knew this may be a permanent move. Minami arrived with a small U-Haul van to get her vanity, vanity chair, and big giant luxury mirror I had gifted her for that memorable twenty-first birthday.

"Halo Gov'nuh!" Minami said in an English accent. She often did that upon entering the house to me. "Halo Luv!" or "Halo Mate!" Today it was "Halo Gov'nuh!"

"Hey, you little shit," I laughed. "How in the *hell* did *you* rent a U-Haul? You are only twenty-one."

I had laid out thick blankets and a comforter to cushion her things in the van, explaining what should come out first, and how her brother and Pops should help unload.

After the perfect kiss on the cheek and watching my "Favorite Little Asian" drive that U-Haul van down my street and around the corner, I felt so fawking super-sad like crazy. Such an empty feeling.

YSC! You're So Cool!

And the next day she was back and every day after. She would just pop in, park in the garage with "her" Range Rover, grab something to eat, and just hang with me.

"Do you miss me, Bret?" she would ask, eating a plate of food while seated at the conference table I have placed in my dining room.

"No, Minami...You are here every day," I answered. "You just don't sleep here anymore."

Minami got serious. "I'm not annoying You?"

"Just get your things and come back." I said.

When her competition bikini arrived in the US Mail, I called her, and she immediately raced to my house. She had just a couple of weeks before competition, and she was set to go. She did not choose to attend the ceremony for her University of New Mexico graduation, but she was sure proud to earn her degree(s) in entrepreneurship, business, and finance...THREE Degrees...Way to go Minami. Such a smarty pants.

Her fitness competition was on a Saturday evening in June, and Cisco, the Maintenance and Engineering manager from our stucco plant, was hired to be the DJ for the event. Cisco and his wife Marla had a successful DJ business on the side, and they arranged to provide me a free pass with lanyard for the event. The year before, Cisco had helped me move a bunch of boxes from a pod storage Minami had rented just prior to her moving into my home, so he had actually met Minami. Cisco instructed me to dress casual, so I wore khaki pants with a crisp white Ralph Lauren Oxford dress shirt, my polished dress cowboy boots, and a dark charcoal-grey jacket with white pocket square. The only other person dressed like me at the event was the MC, and because of that, Cisco tormented me.

Not sure if should even bother telling you...YES, Minami won "First Place 2019 NPC Mid-USA Bikini Novice" as well as "First Place Bikini True Novice." Minami had a lot of fluid in her movements, and she deserved to win. Her body was incredible.

Minami continued to come to my home often, sometimes when I was home, and other times during the day while I was at work. She still went to the gym daily, just not for the hard-core training like before. I invited her for cheesecake.

"I was thinking, Minami," I started. "Do you anything lined up before law school?"

"No…just working shifts at Peaks still for now." She answered. Minami was seated at the conference table I used in my dining room, and I was on the red stool beside the counter.

Here is what I think," I began. "Working at Twin Peaks during college is one thing, but continuing to work at Twin Peaks after you have earned three bachelor's degrees will not impress anyone."

"I know," Minami added. "I am working on getting an adult job."

"How about this idea." I said to her, making eye contact. "Why don't we break off all contact for now, including text messages, until you have a different job and no longer work for Twin Peaks."

"I can quit right now," Minami exclaimed. "I won't even work my shift this Friday night."

I burst out laughing. "I am kidding, Minami. You need money. Take your time, but make that a goal to get a more adult college-associated job."

We both laughed.

Just a few days later, shortly after the Fourth of July holiday, I noticed a small charge at McDonald's on my Wells Fargo Platinum Visa card that I share with Minami. I checked and noticed that particular McDonald's location was at Denver International Airport. *Oh crap, I certainly hope Minami's grandmother in California is okay.* There were no airline tickets charged to the Visa card, so I sent Minami a text to determine if I should dispute the charge.

"I am in Miami Beach with my aunt and grandmother. They sent me a plane ticket. Sorry, I was hungry in Denver and got a smoothie from McDonald's."

We spoke on the phone during the month of July.

"I found a job with a PR firm and at a night club as a server, Bret," Minami told me.

I went to her parent's home and retrieved "her" Range Rover so it could be parked in my garage.

"My family still wants me to go to law school...Are you ready to be stuck with me for three years, Bret?" Minami asked.

"Sure. Bring your things back," I told her.

A few days later, Minami informed me, "I think I just may work her in Miami Beach for a while and start my online CBD business instead of law school."

"Do you need transportation?" I asked. "Do we need to get your Range Rover out there?"

"A road trip with *you* would be so much fun, Bret," Minami giggled.

"It would be just as expensive to send by auto transport." I told her. "It's over nineteen-hundred miles, and that would be nearly a three-days drive. I have driven to New York from Albuquerque and Washington DC there and back...Not much fun and a big strain on a car to drive ten to twelve hours per day."

We researched and made preliminary bids with auto transport companies.

Three different times Minami declined to have me ship "her" Range Rover to Miami Beach. "Since my grandmother and my aunt live in the Los Angeles, California area, they think I should move there and work."

Minami sent me more than one text about coming to Miami Beach to visit. "I know you would love it here, Bret."

"Minami, I am not here to hold you back or to set you free," I boldly told her. "Please do not expect me to validate what *you* want. Only *you* know what is best for *you*."

At a PR Event, Minami met Daymond John, the founder of FUBU and famous from *Shark Tank*. "He said if I am ever on Shark

Tank, he will remember me, Bret!" Minami was so excited.

"The plan is to get my business up and running well...Hire you, Bret, and then you move here to Miami Beach with me," Minami told me in a text.

At the time of my writing of this book, Minami has a flight scheduled back to Albuquerque for the Labor Day weekend. For now she is making some good money in Miami Beach, but her family is convincing her to move to California closer to them. I have informed Minami that I like the Los Angeles deal best, since flights are shorter, and one can actually drive a car from Albuquerque to Los Angeles in just a day.

I will know more when Minami and I have the time to visit and open her birthday presents that have been gift wrapped so nice waiting for her all summer. Minami is now twenty-two years old.

I really hate to leave the reader hanging like this, but this just goes to show that stories never really end. There are no endings... Life just blends into more and more stories. Some are connected and related, and some are just...stories that may or may not have meaning. I have a bunch more wonderful stories to tell. There will be more books from me.

Just so you know...if you read *How to Make a Woman Happy*, that book ended with me getting a subscription of *The Wall Street Journal* sent to my house since Minami needed it for one of her classes.

The Wall Street Journal continues to be delivered to my home each day.

I pride myself in understanding how to KEEP a woman happy.